jewellery design
and development

jewellery design
and development

from concept to object

Norman Cherry

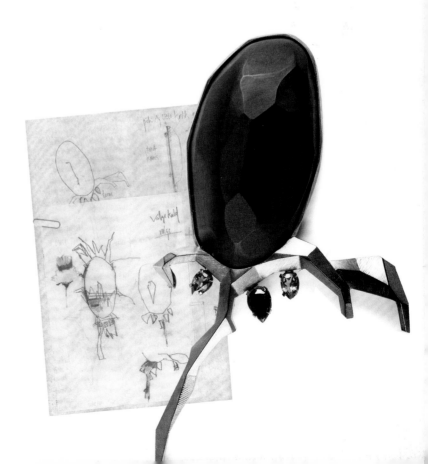

BLOOMSBURY
LONDON · NEW DELHI · NEW YORK · SYDNEY

First published in Great Britain 2013
Bloomsbury Publishing Plc
50 Bedford Square
London WC1B 3DP
www.bloomsbury.com

ISBN: 9781408124970

A CIP catalogue record for this book is
available from the British Library

Commissioning editor: Susan James
Assistant editor: Agnes Upshall
Copy editor: Jane Anson
Cover design: Eleanor Rose
Page design: Elizabeth Healey

This book is produced using paper that is
made from wood grown in managed,
sustainable forests. It is natural, renewable
and recyclable. The logging and
manufacturing processes conform to the
environmental regulations of the country of
origin.

Printed and bound in China

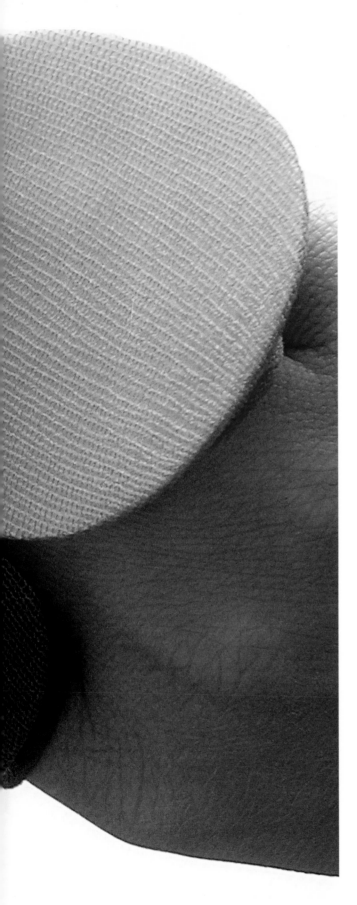

CONTENTS

Preface   6
Note on artists' statements   12
Introduction   13

Artists

Helen Britton   22
Sigurd Bronger   28
Peter Chang   32
Giovanni Corvaja   36
Simon Cottrell   42
Ramon Puig Cuyàs   50
Iris Eichenberg   56
Yoko Izawa   62
Rian de Jong   68
Lisa Juen   74
Kadri Mälk   80
Judy McCaig   86
Ruudt Peters   92
Natalya Pinchuk   98
Peter Skubic   104
Graziano Visintin   110
Mizuko Yamada   114

Afterword   121
Artists' CVs   122
Bibliography   140
Further reading and links   141
Index   142
Picture credits   144

PREFACE

'The relation of word to thought, and the creation of new concepts, is a complex, delicate, and mysterious process'

Leo Tolstoy [1]

Jewellery is one of the oldest art forms, the desire to decorate the body being one of the most basic human instincts. Prehistoric people painted and tattooed their bodies, practices which have continued in many parts of the world to this day. [2] Jewellery as we might recognise it today it has certainly been known since Neanderthal times [3] when cave-dwelling inhabitants of Spain crafted personal ornaments from shells. Brno Man, a well-preserved human specimen from 40,000 BCE, was found near the Czech town, wearing various forms of ornament. [4] The urge to make and wear jewellery seems to have been a more or less continuous activity since those times. Jewellery has denoted rank and warrior status, demonstrated wealth, been a sign of religious membership and hierarchy, of love, of betrothal and marriage, has had magical, talismanic and amuletic properties, has taken the form of seals for legal and other contracts, and for international treaties; it has been used to denote authenticity, to signal good faith, and in many cultures is still a form of portable wealth. Today in most societies it probably demonstrates the cult of personality more than anything, regardless of its value.

Great artists, such as the sixteenth-century Holbein the Younger, designed jewels of one sort or another, as well as depicting them in paintings. Some, like Dürer, a near-contemporary of Holbein, began their careers as engravers and goldsmiths. Hogarth, working a century later, was originally a highly-skilled engraver making commercial copies of other artists' paintings. Cellini wrote a famous treatise which lays as much claim to his self-appointed place in art history as his autobiography. Nicholas Hilliard's miniature portraits of the Elizabethan age are as much jewels as fine art.

In recent times painters and sculptors have been tempted to design jewels. The Americans Art Smith and Alexander Calder were serious about jewellery, Smith being especially influential in the development of the contemporary American movement in the middle of the twentieth century. Margaret de Patta was another American who came to jewellery via fine art and was much influenced and encouraged by the émigré sculptor Moholy-Nagy, who taught her for a time in Chicago. She learned from that experience to appreciate some of the qualities and problems common to jewellery, sculpture and architecture: those of space, form, tension, structure, scale, texture, interpenetration, superimposition, and economy of means.

In Britain, Alan Davie created jewellery for a period around 1949–50 and was an influential teacher at the Central School of Art and Design at about the same time. Picasso's jewellery may be seen as the product of an endlessly curious mind, even in a perhaps less than self-critical old age, while Dalí's quite breathtaking efforts were perhaps as much about his well-developed commercial acumen as his enquiring and uniquely creative practice.

Jewels made from rare precious metals were for centuries the preserve of the wealthy, the aristocracy and royalty. It was not until the Industrial Revolution and the subsequent age of mass production that opportunities first arose for the middle classes and then the masses to purchase more modest forms of personal adornment in precious metals for themselves. In the eighteenth and nineteenth centuries, Berlin Iron Work and Wolverhampton Steel Ware used cut and polished steel to imitate precious materials, the former as a token of investment in Prussian war efforts, the latter simply as cheap copies of more expensive items to enable the working classes to ape their betters. Like many antiques, these now have proportionally far greater worth than their original intrinsic values.

Some of the most interesting, and not especially expensive, examples of jewellery art came out of the Art Nouveau and Arts and Crafts movements at the turn of the twentieth century, when the concept of the

jewellery artist started to grow largely as a result of the inclusion of metalwork and jewellery in the curricula of the still relatively new art schools. Today, the intrinsic value of the materials employed need have no direct bearing on an item's eventual monetary or artistic value, whether the materials are precious, 'alternative' or denote 'bling'. The history of jewellery is a fascinating subject which has been well documented by many talented and knowledgeable historians with far greater depth of expertise than I. There is a vast number of informative and interesting books on the subject, so there would be little reason in this volume to cover ground already so well and effectively trodden, tempting as it might be.

However, it is true that since the craft revolution that took place in the 1970s and 1980s, jewellery has changed out of all recognition. As the excitement, confidence, and rebelliousness of the sixties superseded the caution and tradition of the dreary, war-weary fifties, there was a sense of change throughout most of Western society. Once the 1968 generation of revolutionary students had overturned many of the conventions and accepted notions of higher education across all subjects, but especially in the visual arts, it was inevitable that what constituted jewellery would, as with other art forms, be subject to its own revision. Students were no longer subjected to a traditional 'academic' education in which they learned by studying classical examples and were instructed in a traditionally didactic manner. Rather, their natural enquiring impulses were encouraged – or at least initially accepted – and boring, repetitive exercises were no longer undertaken. Without realising it, perhaps, the concept of the student as individual researcher and explorer after new knowledge had begun.

What materials were acceptable or accepted, what actually constituted jewellery *per se*, became the subject of debate. Young jewellers began to experiment with non-precious metals, and with other 'soft' materials. Recycling was common, especially of ephemeral material such as the pages of unwanted or used books, theatre, cinema and bus tickets, as was the incorporation of other found objects and material. Some of the new plastics became popular, as did refractory metals such as titanium, tantalum, and niobium, all of which could be coloured either electrolytically or by the use of a hot flame – in great contrast to the relatively monotonal qualities of the precious metals hitherto regarded as sacrosanct. Stainless steel was favoured by some, and the beginnings of consumer product miniaturisation in the form of watch and camera batteries made it possible to power wearable miniature kinetic pieces.

Questions of intrinsic value became linked to the philosophical debates taking place. As Warhol and others raised questions of value and understanding of Art with a capital A, what seemed like an army of philosophers, critics and writers were beginning to suggest that what constituted art was as much to do with how the viewer saw and understood it rather than what any 'rules' told us we should think. If the artist offered a work of art and a viewer accepted it as art, then it must be art. And so followed the crafts, albeit in more modest fashion. But within the field, the debate was lively and challenging. The body became not just the receptacle or vehicle for display of jewellery objects: for some artists it was the jewellery, for others this approach to jewellery led to experiments with clothing, while some fashion designers were at much the same time creating clothes with a more structured look, almost sculptural in effect.

Some jewellers were influenced by theatre and architecture, especially le Coq's 'Theatre of Movement' in Paris, and jewellery for them was an extension of the body, an investigation of its relationship to the space around it. Jewellery had become a form of performance art.

Dutch jewellers were very much at the forefront of this questioning and experimenting, closely followed by the Germans and British. In the USA, the practice of jewellery has not developed as it has in Britain or Europe, where we can trace a more or less continuous line back through history. There were few higher education programmes until immediately after the Second World War when the GI Bill gave grants to returning service personnel to study. In addition, a programme of Occupational Therapy for returning veterans included subjects like pottery and jewellery. With such a different genesis, it is no wonder that American jewellery was always much freer from constraint and preconceived rules or prejudices.

As Graham Hughes' 1961 landmark exhibition 'Modern Jewellery 1890–1961' at Goldsmiths' Hall in London awakened the public to the possibilities offered by a new contemporary view of jewellery as design, so the Crafts Council's 'The Jewellery Project' of 1983, 'Cross Currents' which toured in Britain and Australia during 1983–84, followed by Ralph Turner and Peter Dormer's 'The New Jewellery – Trends and Traditions' in 1985 shocked the public into reconsidering what jewellery actually was. It is from that background that we view jewellery today.

The subject of this book – how contemporary jewellers create their works – is not about the design of jewellery as commercial product. It is about jewellery as creative studio practice. Jewellery is arguably one of the most vibrant, exciting and challenging contemporary art forms. It is relatively small in scale, compact, wearable and therefore portable. It can tell a story about the wearer or bearer, about that person's family or background, about personality. It may be a demonstration of wealth, although often enough in contemporary jewellery the materials are not intrinsically precious. Each piece of jewellery tells a story in its own way. But there is usually some sort of underlying history, often untold, about its own creation, about the materials used or found, about the influences on the artist who generated the idea, developed it, and finally made the piece what it is. Above all, it is an art form which is readily accessible to most of us, regardless of our financial status, for some contemporary jewellery is surprisingly inexpensive, given the power of the statement it can make.

How artists, and especially jewellery artists, generate and develop ideas has long been a preoccupation of mine. As a practising jeweller myself, I have several approaches which vary from project to project and depend on differing circumstances at any given time. As an educator (and today the teacher is very much an enabler and encourager, sometimes a 'co-producer', rather than a didactic master with pupils in the *atelier*),

I am aware of needing to lay down a groundwork of guidance and general methodology, an understanding of critical practice, theory, and history, which educates, encourages and enables students to analyse, to research, to develop their own creative approaches to the subject and to be able to evaluate the end products of their labours. Indeed, there are so many different 'jewelleries' that it might be said that there must inevitably be just as many 'methodologies'.

Having discussed the subject with many of my fellow jewellers over the years, I realised that most of them had the same questions in mind, and we all had different 'answers' – if that is even the right word to use. It could be said that designers address 'problems' for which they seek practical solutions, while artists, in a spirit of open-ended enquiry, pose questions or present situations to an audience to provoke debate and discussion.

So, when the idea for this book first arose, I decided to take advice from some of the best and most interesting practitioners working today and invite them to share their thoughts. Precisely whom to ask was particularly difficult: there are so very many innovative, creative, thoughtful, challenging and highly talented jewellers practising today. Could I be truly objective? In these circumstances what exactly would constitute 'objectivity'? Should I try to establish categories and, if so, how or what? Were there national or regional characteristics to be recognised? The more I thought about the idea of categorisation, it became evident that some artists would qualify for more than one notional category and, indeed, might not even agree with their eventual categorisation in any case. I informally asked a number of colleagues about definitions of categories and no two could actually agree. Having been rather strangely and mystifyingly categorised myself in one particular publication, I came to the conclusion that any attempt to do so would be an entirely false construct and counterproductive. Similarly, in such a truly international age I find it harder and harder to recognise truly national characteristics any more.

Eventually I made the decision to simply ask those artists whose work I like and admire, whose work is intriguing, challenging, and emphatically exemplifies an individual philosophy, to take part. Therefore, the choice of collaborators is entirely partisan, tempered only by the constraints on space. Consequently this book illustrates the work and thoughts of a range of jewellers including the well-established, the mid-career, and some emerging members of our profession. They come from several countries and cultures. All demonstrate creativity of a high order, thoughtfulness and, especially, a deep passion for what they do. I am very grateful to them for sharing their thoughts with me, for taking the time and trouble to document the process of creating a particular piece or group of jewellery for this book, and for being generous enough to agree to putting what are often very private moments into the public domain: one can feel very exposed in doing so. So, to my seventeen colleagues featured in this work, I owe a debt of gratitude.

I have learnt a great deal from looking at, reading about and, of course, discussing the project with all the participants over the past three years, and I hope very much that readers will find the experience as useful, inspiring, and rewarding as I have.

Whether you read this book as a student, a teacher, a curator or critic, as a collector, a fellow professional, or simply out of general interest, may you enjoy the experience and feel more informed as a result.

Norman Cherry

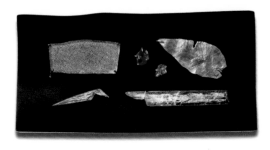

NOTE ON ARTISTS' STATEMENTS

When I asked each artist for a statement about their individual approaches to creating jewellery, I suggested an 'ideal' length. It was not an instruction, just an indication of what would be ideal in terms of words related to space available: advisorial. Inevitably that 'advice' was interpreted in widely varying ways; some artists have been economical with words and very much to the point in what they have said, while others have been more expansive. I was faced with a decision: whether to edit these statements down to a standard length and risk losing much of the intention and sense of what artists are telling us, or accept that each will have a different amount of space. I decided, with the kind agreement of my editor, that it was better to suffer from some irregularity in space allocation than to lose the essence of what individuals are saying about their practice.

Similarly, some artists supplied many more illustrations than can be reasonably fitted into this volume; others felt that relatively few explained what they had done. So, on balance the decision was that, while we wish to give a similar amount of space to all the artists, we should nevertheless not reduce the impact of the 'story' by unduly reducing the number of visuals. My thanks are due to both editor and book designer for the sensitivity and creativity with which they undertook this task.

INTRODUCTION

When the seventeen artists agreed to take part in this book I was very excited to know that I would be able to share their individual creative philosophies with our readers. While I expected seventeen different, very personal, approaches, nevertheless, having my own particular ways of creating jewellery, I naturally imagined that most other jewellers might work in a fairly similar manner. For me, drawing has always been an integral part of the process. I often record day-to-day observations and notes in a sketchbook and sometimes refer to these to work through ideas, using drawing as a generational and developmental tool, recording thoughts and manipulating these as I go, seeking to improve and change, exploring several variations, always searching for the ideas which will take me confidently to the bench where I then work with the materials in the next stage of the journey towards an eventual solution. However, it is not always necessarily a formal activity done in a sketchbook or at a drawing board in the studio: often fleeting ideas are jotted down on agendas and documents during meetings, in a notebook while travelling, on a menu or table napkin at dinner or lunch, and so on. Sometimes, drawings from another time are remembered or rediscovered, mentally manipulated, developed, and interpreted in metals. Sometimes I work directly with the materials, responding to their feel and how they react, moving component parts around on the bench this way and that, stopping, starting, reversing, rearranging, 'reframing the problem', until the moment when they have somehow reached that point of compositional balance when I know somehow to stop; but I am pretty certain that when I do this it is informed by some earlier drawing activity, filed away in a more or less indefinable 'library of ideas' which can be drawn on unexpectedly.

For most jewellery artists the actual methodology we use for creating is not a step-by-step process rigidly adhered to at all times. We are not Scientific Positivists after all, for whom everything is a matter of strictly laid-out procedures designed to produce a particular set of outcomes according to a tightly written hypothesis, when pre-existing knowledge leads to actions and outcomes. We are not working to a blueprint which must be carried out to the nearest few microns. I would go as far as to say that the majority of artists are often not, perhaps never, conscious of the steps they are following in order to create a piece. Much of what we do is instinctive, a kind of visceral process: something that just has to be done. It is only after the event, when we think about it – or more likely are asked about it by someone else – that we can actually rationalise it. The period of creation is usually quite frenetic, exciting, almost 'white hot', with only one thing on our minds – the jewellery, the art: this is described by David Pye as 'complete concentration of the mind' for 'quite short periods of time'.[5]

It is what might be described by some theorists as 'reflection in action' when the artist is making continuous decisions based on experience, knowledge, self-knowledge, informed by previous similar, but different, projects.[6] Decision-making is based on something which cannot be easily explained, in much the same way that a musician might make continuous minor adjustments to phrasing, intonation, to fingering, or a sportsman to grip or stance, which have not been planned or thought about in advance.[7] These are responses to the constantly changing situation or circumstances. When a specific adjustment is made to the proportion, or the texture, or the component parts of a piece of jewellery, the decision is not merely capricious or felicitous. It is a result of the 'know-how' which is 'in the action'.[8] Perhaps the material does not respond as expected, as it has thousands of times before, perhaps a surface or a combination of elements suddenly seems to offer unexpected qualities or opportunities, or a particular material looks or feels such that it invites doing something unexpected or unplanned with it. It is the experience and tacit knowledge of the jeweller which takes over often enough, rather than a conscious pause to consider these 'new' circumstances and make a formal decision on how to proceed. Most of the artists in this study describe it simply as 'intuitive'.

Creating jewellery, like most other art forms, is a continuous engagement with an intuitive process which results from an accumulation of visual, theoretical, technical, personal and other factors – intuition based on implicit or tacit knowledge: research in action, reflective practice, improvisation. This is a way of thinking recognised by several writers and commentators on creativity in the visual arts and, perhaps surprisingly, to some of the sciences. Dr Chris O'Toole, a prominent entomologist, described making creative decisions based on a virtually unconscious assimilation of great swathes of information over very short periods of time. He referred in one public lecture to 'the jizz – the moment when a sort of realisation dawns … and the accumulation of years of study and observation, knowledge, and experience enables you to recognise it instantly'.[9] This is not dissimilar to the theorist and teacher Krome Barratt referring to 'knowingness': a sort of Cartesian assimilation of all the relevant information we might need for the (often unexpected) insight which results in something new and original.[10]

That 'knowingness' comes in part from a sort of library of visual knowledge and related practical experience accrued over the years – what Barratt describes as the human propensity to want to find out things; what might be described by some as 'useless information', i.e. all manner of information that interests us at some point and which we read, watch, see, listen to, record (often unconsciously), and somehow remember, but which has no immediate or obvious use at the time. At some stage, however, we dredge it up – or perhaps it just somehow presents itself to us – and it informs and influences the work in hand.[11] Therefore, it must be said that there can be no such thing as 'useless knowledge'. We are naturally curious as human beings and our curiosity is inherently useful.

During the creative process we are constantly asking ourselves 'what if?' 'why?' 'could?' 'should?' and so

on: consciously or unconsciously. The answers to those questions – which I think are actually fundamental to the creator – are often equally unconsciously provided. Such is the actuality, the reality, of reflexive practice.

In the examples which follow in this book, most of the artists refer to working directly with materials, experimenting with components, arranging and rearranging parts until a harmonious solution is arrived at. This is arguably a form of three-dimensional drawing in itself: drawing through materials, so to speak. Indeed, one of the artists talks about the manipulation of materials actually being the drawing process in itself. Others draw conventionally throughout the process, refining and developing ideas as they go. Still others use drawing at some stage or other, yet feel that the contact with the materials is by far the most important factor in their creative process. Materiality is what drives them.

For some artists Computer Aided Design (CAD) has become an invaluable tool. In some cases this is simply because the particular software employed can take a lot of the drudgery of idea development out of the process and speed it up immensely; for others it can almost instantly create diagrammatical and technical forms which might otherwise have taken many hours to do by conventional technical drawing or, in some cases, through intuitive and investigative, but somewhat imprecise, soft model making, such as the use of paper, card, clay or plasticine. Sometimes the artist finds it difficult to envisage a complex but viable three-dimensional form by freehand drawing and CAD has come to the rescue to enable the realisation of a good idea which otherwise might never have seen the light of day.

Nevertheless, for all of them the materials with which they work are paramount. This is very much a haptic experience rather than simply a process *per se*. Not for them the automatic production of an idea completely worked out in advance and interpreted like a detailed assembly drawing given to a technician to follow as closely and accurately as possible. This is not miniature engineering. No matter how well each has envisaged an idea, its structure, its shape, its colour scheme, textures, decoration, or finishes, it is a given that the proposed object will change in some way or another as it begins to take form in the studio and become a *something*, as it goes through the process of *poiesis*: passing from the state of not being to being, making the unseen (an

idea) into the seen (the jewellery). This is jewellery as art form, not jewellery as commercial artefact, produced to a formula. (Of course, well-designed contemporary jewellery produced in mass or in batch production has its place in society and in our economy, but it is not what this book is interested in.)

As ideas develop and a work begins to take shape on the bench, often new possibilities present themselves, unforeseen difficulties or interesting problems arise. Sometimes these are visual, sometimes technical, intellectual, or practical. The artist is constantly faced with this changing landscape of creative activity, with the need or the desire, maybe even just the temptation, to 'reframe the problem' without knowing the outcome.[12] All of this requires a level of sensitivity that comes out of the reflection and practice that informs and inspires the making: thinking adaptively rather than logically, as Plotkin put it so elegantly.[13] None of this comes easily or quickly. It is the result of reflexive practice which most definitely requires patience and long-term application. Richard Sennett in his book *The Craftsman* talks of the 10,000-hour rule, by which he maintains that anyone whom he defines as a craftsman (he includes *inter alia* sportsmen, surgeons, jazz musicians, and composers within this definition) does not reach a level of true expertise until they have undergone around 10,000 hours of practice. [14] That may at first glance seem excessive, but it might just be worth musing on that figure and, regardless of your background, think of your own experience so far and where you are in your career; or think of the professionals in almost any field whom you most admire for their expertise. How much practice does an individual have to undertake in order to become a consummate professional, a real expert: a top athlete, musician, gymnast, a consultant surgeon, a seriously good jeweller? How long did it take to learn something simple like sawing a circle from a sheet of metal without breaking a blade, to solder a clean joint almost without thinking about it? How long does it take to learn to generate an idea and develop it through to a satisfactory conclusion?

Once you have technical command of your medium you are free to experiment, to explore the previously perceived boundaries and navigate well beyond them. Reaching such levels of expertise is about training – self-training as often as not, and the self-discipline which goes with that. In the way that the athlete undergoes a daily regime in order to improve fitness, speed, endurance, so the jeweller might be expected to practise particular technical skills until they are executed just as unconsciously as breathing. Creative skills usually develop in much the same way. Few artists are born ready made, not even the Greats. I believe that Picasso was credited with saying that his art was ninety per cent perspiration and ten per cent inspiration, although that aphorism has also been attributed to Thomas Edison about a hundred years before. Another great twentieth-century artist, Augustus John, once described painting as 'sheer hell' until the work was completed. Lucian Freud was known to sometimes spend years on a painting until he was completely satisfied that it was at last 'right'.

There has been in recent years some debate around the concept of 'slow' craft as opposed to 'fast', by which some protagonists have suggested that the essence of craft is in the slowness and thoroughness of the whole process as opposed to speed of execution. The opposing view has, perhaps with a sense of mischief, suggested ways of undertaking what I can best describe as 'instant' craft. The older I become, the more convinced I am that there are many more questions than answers, and that many such 'credos' are inherently untrustworthy. Sometimes work can indeed be done very quickly, apparently instantly; if it is good work rather than facile, the maker has most likely spent many years learning and practising, and accruing very high levels

of thinking and making skills so that good results do sometimes happen apparently effortlessly. Whatever else, good work is good work.

A good knowledge of theory as well as practice is also necessary for the accumulation of the skills required to be a contemporary creative jewellery artist. As Sennett shows, skill is about an interrelationship between thinking and doing practised over several years. He talks about 'material consciousness' and 'how it feels'. He talks about intuition and the 'intuitive leap'. It is what he calls 'a special form of induction'.[15] Donald Schön describes what he calls 'knowing in action' as almost indefinable, intuitive processes such as 'thinking on your feet', 'finding the groove', 'a feel for the music', and 'feel for the ball',[16] like Sennett, using sportsmen and jazz musicians as examples of professionals who, like artists and designers, are reflexive practitioners *par excellence*. Most of the jewellers I know believe strongly in the interrelationship of theory and practice – *praxis* – but I doubt very much if any of them think about it consciously as they work in the studio.

No matter what our levels of visual, thinking, and technical skills, no matter what our specialist area of activity, what we all have in common is the most important sense next to sight – the haptic. The haptic sense as part of our learning process is in danger of being lost to a large extent in contemporary life as we become more and more involved with and almost inseparable from, the digital. We cannot live without our mobile phones, our computers, our iPods, our need to be able to communicate instantly, to do things faster and faster and apparently more effectively. How many students today can use software to work faster than ever before, taking the drudgery out of large parts of the design process? Yet how many actually fully understand what it is that they are doing? Without the experience of actually touching and manipulating materials, whether they are metals, plastics, fabric, stone, paper or pencil, how do we really know what will or can happen to them, how they react, what we can or cannot do with them? For most people today, the most touch-sensitive experience they ever have is their fingertips on a computer keyboard, the keypad of a mobile phone, or the screen of their iPad.

Studies have demonstrated that a major part of the development of young children is due to touching and doing, and learning to relate that to what they see[17] –

by the age of five months the arm has learned, under the guidance of the eye, to move towards a target object, and by ten months the hand is able to shape itself ready to grasp it. And so the hand/eye relationship becomes ever more complex as the child grows and learns. Yet modern education, perforce, obliges them to have less and less of that experience as they get older. We consider it an achievement that under-fives can use computers and some even have their own mobile phones. Electronic consumer items are increasingly being designed and mass produced specifically for toddlers. This is seen as an advancement in education and in our evolution, yet that very haptic sense which we all seem to need so much is progressively denied them.

Education in the crafts has shrunk immensely over the past twenty years to the extent that very few programmes of study at university level now employ the word 'crafts' in their title, so embarrassing and backward is it considered in many HE circles. This seems to be directly related to the fact that state-funded secondary schools have virtually abandoned any form of real craftwork, especially for 12–18-year-olds. Consequently those wishing to study art and design at university level have much less idea of what the 'craft' subjects – ceramics, glass, jewellery, or textiles – might entail. The interest and the growth are in areas which use ICT. Even programmes which used to employ direct model making, such as Product Design, are now more likely to be largely digitally based. Industrial demand is proven for graduates in areas such as Electronic Arts, Media, Moving Image, and Digital Design.

I am neither a Luddite nor a technophobe, but in fact an enthusiastic proponent of the use of CAD and CADCAM. Indeed I played a major part in the introduction and development of several aspects of CADCAM, especially Rapid Prototyping, and the use of lasers, to the British jewellery field, as long ago as 1997 when, as Head of the Birmingham School of Jewellery, I set up the Jewellery Industry Innovation Centre. I do not believe that we should fear or deny new technologies, especially those which make it easier or quicker for us to create. Many leading designers and jewellery artists have embraced these new technologies with vigour and with great success, and view them as simply new tools to be used creatively. So, in a sense, CADCAM is no different from other processes such as raising, engraving, or casting, enabling us to create things and forms we

might not have been able to make previously. It can be an excellent aid to creativity. That cannot in itself be bad.

But what does concern me is that, quite understandably, government policy makers in most advanced countries nowadays wish to encourage young people in education to learn the skills which they perceive in their unfortunately limited and unimaginative way will most benefit the economy, so ICT has assumed a very important status within education, and understandably so. A well-educated workforce proficient in ICT is essential to an advanced economy. In most economically advanced countries the currently prevailing educational philosophies seem to favour technological, intellectual, conceptual, and verbal creativities over the practical. Activity which is perceived as 'handwork' is considered to be backward, redolent of a past when industrial productivity and national economies were dependant on a prospective workforce learning high levels of hand skills. However, the perhaps unintentional result of this is that we have discarded other aspects of educational development which are actually much more crucial to young people's development than we realise. This is not part of some great international conspiracy, it is just a result of uninformed policy-making by people who are not in themselves creative and do not always understand

the realities – or the unintended consequences – of their decisions, while genuinely convinced of the need to encourage creative thinking and action of a particular sort in a contemporary society. The battles fought generations ago by Dewey and others[18] for the value of craft as an educational tool and not just a means of vocational training for less academically-able children, have been consigned to the rubbish heap of history.

For those of us for whom making is an expression of our thoughts, our consciousness, our way of life, our interpretation of humanity, our creative contribution to society, this is a potentially disastrous state of affairs. Science and Technology make life possible, but it is the Arts and Humanities which interpret it, which make it bearable, enjoyable, and worthwhile. Where will future generations of makers come from if there is no meaningful materials-based education at secondary school level? It seems a great pity that pre-school education and elementary schools do such a marvellous job of developing young people's creativity and thinking through the exploration of materials and processes, for that to be ignored during the next six years, precisely when teenagers are deciding what careers to follow. The redesignation of crafts education as 'Design and Technology' and the consequent reduction of craft work in many secondary schools to what I might describe as 'designing by numbers' is serving young people badly and denying them valuable learning opportunities and experiences. We might wish that education decision-makers would pay more attention to the views of Sir Ken Robinson, the influential and much-admired advocate for the creative arts as a major learning experience,[19] but so far none have been brave or insightful enough to put his theories into practice.

Perhaps it is not really surprising then that university art departments and schools regularly receive applications from middle-aged career changers seeking to retrain for a second, or even third, career which will offer more immediate intellectual satisfaction as they learn to think creatively through doing and making. Perhaps the phenomenon of 'rough' craft, DIY, and the renewed interest in hand knitting originating out of amateur and semi-professional crafts activity are other manifestations of that human need to interpret life through the thinking medium of our hands. Is it only coincidental that much of the impact of Tracey Emin and some of the other 'Young British Artists' was related to their slightly 'rough and ready' craft approach to their art? They do actually make things. Emin's embroideries are certainly not fine craft works, nor could some of the wooden structures she has created be described as anything other than rough, make-do joinery, but she does seem to have ignited an interest in making *per se*. The work has a sense of having been thought through as it was made.

The Finnish architect and theorist Juhani Pallasmaa believes that knowledge and experience of materials are not just craftwork in the sense of unthinking quotidian manual work, but an intellectual activity, that making is a process of thinking with the hands which leads to innovation and creativity.[20] Kant's idea of the hands as a window of the mind suggests that the hand is a conduit for information that modifies our thinking and how we do things.[21] Frank Wilson, an eminent American neuroscientist who in recent years has been enthusiastically working with visionary educators who

use the arts to engage and improve the life chances of so-called delinquent adolescents, believes that the hand is not just connected to the brain but can quite reasonably be considered a part of it.[22] He informs us in his book *The Hand* that the skin and tips of the thumb and forefinger are treated by the brain in much the same way as the macula – the most sensitive part of the retina. [23] Initially the eye searches for and finds an object which the hand then explores, but increasingly the hand will do the finding and, in my opinion, the thinking.

The 'thinking hand' is a well-established concept in all craft circles, not least among jewellers. High levels of skill come about through many years of thinking and doing. [24] It is clear to me that the seventeen jewellery artists featured in this book are all excellent examples of people with hands that think, question and do: hands which perhaps know more than any of us can say.[25]

REFERENCES

1. Tolstoy, L. (1903) *Pedagogical Writings* cited in L. Vygotsky, Thought and Language (Vygotsky's own translation (1934) revised and edited by A. Kozulin [1986]). Cambridge, MA: MIT Press. p. 151

2. Caplan, J. ed. (2000) *Written on the Body*. London: Reaktion Books. p. xv

3. Lambert, S. (1998) *The Ring. Design: Past and Present*. Crans–près–Céligny, Switzerland. p. 19

4. Balter, M. (15 January 2010) *Neandertal Jewelry Shows Their Symbolic Smarts*. Science. Vol. 327, issue 5963 pp. 255–256

5. Pye, D. (1978) *The Nature and Aesthetics of Design*. London: The Herbert Press. p. 38

6. Schön, D. (1991) *The Reflective Practitioner, How Professionals Think in Action*. Aldershot: Ashgate Publishing. p. 50

7. Ibid. p. 54

8. Ibid. p. 50

9. O'Toole, C. (1999) *Feed the Fury*. [Conference at University of Oxford Museum of Natural History] November

10. Barratt, K. (1989) *Logic and Design*. New York: Design Press. p. 302

11. Ibid. p. 302

12. Schön, D., op. cit. p. 134

13. Plotkin, H. (1993) *Darwin, Machines and the Nature of Knowledge*. Cambridge, MA: Harvard University Press. pp. 190–198

14. Sennett, R. (2008) *The Craftsman*. London: Allen Lane. p. 20

15. Ibid. p. 212

16. Schön, D., op. cit. p. 54

17. Wilson, F. R. (1998) *The Hand*. New York: Pantheon Books. p. 99

18. Adamson, G. (2007) *Thinking Through Craft*. Oxford: Berg. p. 83

19. Robinson, K. (2011) *Out of Our Minds: Learning to be Creative*. Hoboken: Wiley.

20. Snell, T. (2010) Public Lecture. '*Good Design – Designing Tomorrow*'. Perth, Australia: Jewellers and Metals Guild of Australia.

21. Ibid

22. Wilson, F. R. personal conversation. July 2006.

23. Wilson, op. cit. p. 97

24. Sennett, R., op. cit. p. 38

25. Schön, op. cit. p. 51

HELEN BRITTON

STUDIO PHILOSOPHY
The intention has always been to save and preserve, an affirmation to protect and enhance life that is, to announce life to come.

Helen Britton is an Australian living and working in Munich. In an almost indefinable way her jewellery seems to reflect that mix of post-colonial near-exoticism and German cultural hothouse. She brings together the practicalities of sound technique and an uncompromisingly deep aesthetic reflection. The work she has chosen to describe is a wonderful mixture of found items and manufactured bits, held together with a refined sensitivity to materials and aided by judicious, but never unnecessary, use of drawing. She has the ability to see a kind of beauty in the mundane, constructing a 'new' personal sense of what is valued. She describes an ability to see jewel-like potential in flotsam and jetsam, to take inspiration from these and the almost magical quality of the surroundings – the air, the smells, the place itself – to make sense of the apparent chaos, and to ultimately organise that chaos and transform these materials and reactions through time into desirable and inspiring works of art. In effecting this transformation, she questions what we in society actually value, subverting many of our common prejudices as she does so.

On other occasions she is capable of using and subverting traditional jewellery techniques such as conventional claw settings to create very wearable and desirable brooches which are set with plastics as well as semi-precious stones, thereby overturning the whole concept of what is precious and desirable, and what is not. It is very clear from looking at Britton's work that she has a deep love of materials. The collection of other people's castoffs and found objects which she keeps hidden away is described as if it has anthropomorphic qualities: she talks, for example, about 'their oily smile' and 'the giggle of plastics'. I do not think this work has anything to do with a need to shock, but rather it is about using the materials and the new forms and purposes, even personalities, which they assume to communicate through being seen and being actively worn. If the objects do surprise or even shock some beholders, then that must be all to the good. Perhaps such unsuspecting viewers will experience a transformation not unlike that of these previously unwanted materials.

BELOW
Worktable, plastics from cove, general creative chaos and beginnings of necklace.

OPPOSITE
Cove, Queensland, Australia.

HELEN BRITTON

I was on one of those long, white, hot, lonely, but rapidly disappearing coastlines in Queensland, half way up the state. Not much to find washed up, deep ocean close to shore. Then, climbing over a headland, I discovered a little cove, full – stuffed full in fact – with pumice and plastic fragments on what was otherwise a pristine coast. The colours drew me down like lollies. I experience colour as a sensation in the mouth and I have always collected things. Apparently my room smelled of all the fragile, broken and sometimes not quite so dead, lost little lives of the sea creatures I obsessively brought home since the murkiest depths of my childhood. Even now as I write I am aware of the pungent odour of the string I have been trying to dye with the flesh of tiny dead snails whose purple colour works on me like a drug. I am telling you this to simply illustrate how my work began, and still begins every time. I never limited my collecting to the sea shore, there were the beetles, the leaves, the little dried frogs, the glass fragments, the old plastic beads, the discarded clothes, the dug-up bottles, the horse shoes my grandfather had made, whiskers of cats, maggoty seahorses, the list had no end.

The intention has always been to save and preserve, an affirmation to protect and enhance life that is, to announce life to come; an imperative to organise space and materials. I didn't realise I was making art, but this is how it is described by Elizabeth Gross, and she should know: 'Art works through and as materiality but it is the event of sensation and its autonomous life that transforms a random material composition into Art.' And I guess that is in fact what I do.

That I make jewellery, drawings, and paper objects and not fun rides, buildings or gardens is a good thing, because I am building in a way a very private world, that accepts no compromises. To enfold matter into itself, to transform it in unpredictable ways, comes out of a love of materials, out of a sensation of pleasure in simple qualities: colour, texture, form, and their effect on my senses.

I always had empathy for objects, feeling sad for the discarded, the broken, and abused things of the everyday. In my jewellery practice in recent years, I have become more specifically interested in collecting those awkward and sometimes ugly fragments, those hidden beauties, those components that were intended for life as jewellery. I try to provide them with a new opportunity, a chance to sing again or to sing at last. I have a great clamouring collection, all demanding attention, each one such a handful that I keep them tucked away, restless in their boxes, waiting for their day to shine. It is their oily smile, their rugged gesture, the thrust of their metal, the giggle of the plastics, the wink of glass, the jungle of material emotions locked in these fragments, that I am looking to give room for expression.

My work has never been about wanting to affront, react against or shock: I love my materials too much. In the stuff I gather to work with, I recognise the very human desire to make a signal, to communicate, with the intention or hope that someone may be ready, may even find it very necessary, to take this tiny sign, place it on their body, be prepared to have this merge with their self-image and to then present this to the world, in an ancient act both intimate and shared. This is the specificity of jewellery. Jewellery first really becomes jewellery when it is worn. Then there are all the subsequent logistical intricacies of the production of these various components, including my contribution, the materials from which they are made, the machinery they require, the conditions of their production, their trajectories around the planet, their histories. And these processes are also sources of wonder. I see this all around me, and it is this continuous transformation, these great flows of matter and ideas, of chaos and organisation and their relative speeds, that bring about a genuinely intense fascination.

But back to the beach and the piece whose birth I am here making public. I grew up on these Australian beaches and homesickness knows no mercy. I started making work with discarded plastics over twenty years ago. I now live in Germany, with its very different tides of matter and ideas. In between, I have travelled a diverse network of intersecting paths that form the fabric of my practice. When I found this little graveyard of coloured fragments, I knew it was time to trace my way again along the bleached and sandy thread of my beginnings. I wanted to make a piece as sharp and spiky as the bush around the cove, as bleached as the favourite old shirt that I was wearing, and as brittle and fragile as the plastic fragments that I gathered on that remote spot. I wanted to make something to capture the beauty of that whole moment. I wanted to anchor the whole experience in the piece, the smell, the heat of the sun, the scratchy bright environment, everything. My work is always a response to the things I see. I am constantly gathering or photographing or drawing. This is what my work must contain, and it is first when the piece is finished that I can see if it can give me that back. When the piece has enough autonomy to shout out and show me something, then it is finished and free to go into the world on its own trajectory. My practice is always an attempt to connect with the force of experience, to understand the intensity and sensation of experience again, without being engulfed. A big ask for a piece of jewellery, but that is the aim when I make my work. So now you know.

Helen Britton

BELOW
"Crash" ring. Silver, diamonds, paint.

OPPOSITE
"Daytime" brooch. Silver, shells, silk, paint.

SIGURD BRONGER

STUDIO PHILOSOPHY
I tend to get my inspiration from the things I see around me: architecture, art, history, and from listening to music.

BELOW
"A device for wearing a goose egg." Goose egg shell, gold-plated brass, steel, cotton cord.

OPPOSITE
A drawer in my workbench containing some of the different materials I use in my work.

Sigurd Bronger lives and works in Oslo, where he divides his time between his studio and working as a highly skilled technician for the state broadcasting company NRK. By undertaking this paid work he sets himself free from the commercial and other demands of having to make work for anyone other than himself. His principal concern is his relationship with the work itself, not with a potential customer. He says that each time he begins work on a new piece his approach is different, according to the circumstances. He seems to have a variety of modi operandi, but exploratory drawings are always the initial starting point, leading to some sort of idea which can then be examined and interrogated in more detail at the bench. Here his innate technical facility and affinity with materials take over the creative process to a large extent, enabling him to develop ideas without unnecessary constraints. He mentions several activities that inspire him and which often inform the preliminary drawings: from communing with nature (in my experience Norwegians as a nation are very environmentally aware and committed to outdoor pursuits) to non-mainstream rock music. The 'Canterbury Scene' bands were usually a complex mix of rock/jazz/free improvisation and, in the case of Egg, also influenced by neo-classical composers such as Stravinsky. Sigurd's aesthetic certainly seems to be both organic and mechanistic. It is free, unexpected, challenging, humorous, yet contained and refined. The piece featured here makes use of an organic object of great fragility held in a framework which might be best described as a kind of machine, made with great accuracy and technical mastery, a fine piece of miniature engineering in itself. You get the impression that, no matter how instinctive or spontaneous the initial inspiration and unrestricted the early stages of exploration, Sigurd is never in any doubt about his technical ability to carry out any idea which his brain begins to develop and refine.

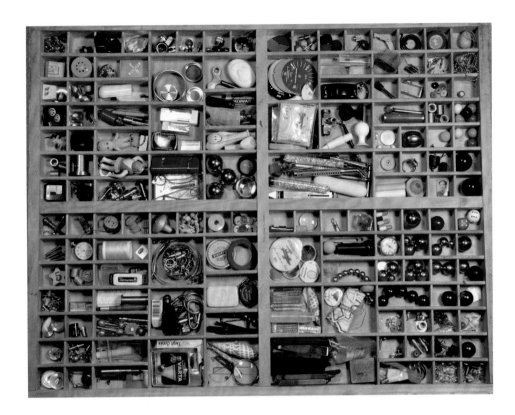

SIGURD BRONGER

A SKETCH OF SOME THOUGHTS ABOUT MY WORKING PROCESS

Often when I am looking for inspiration I will go on walks more or less without apparent purpose and look around me almost like a stranger, a visitor to a landscape which in reality I know well: I experience feelings of freedom, of meaning or, sometimes, lack of meaning, of surprise, of joy and even of a kind of poetry in my physical surroundings. This is when I really observe where I am and find that consequently discoveries simply seem to reveal themselves to me.

Every time I begin a project I have a different approach to how I start my working process.

Of course, it depends on what kind of concept and idea I might have in my mind. Sometimes I will start by making simple sketches on paper and then develop ideas out of those drawings. At a certain stage, which may be different each time, I may

ABOVE
"Turbine" necklace.

OPPOSITE, TOP
"Wearing device for an ostrich egg."

OPPOSITE, BOTTOM, FROM TOP
LEFT
Materials used to construct the
necklace.
Sketching some ideas before
starting work with the materials.
Making two different parts of the
device on the lathe.
Four stages of placing the egg in the
constructed device.

make a model in metal or some other material that I think will be suitable for the particular concept. Other times I go direct to sketching in the material I want to use. By this, I mean that I work directly with the material, using my knowledge, experience, and a certain level of intuition to gradually develop an object. Sketching directly in the material like this takes a lot of patience and concentration. I am calling on a bank of existing knowledge gradually built up over many years. It is not unusual that I might make two or three completely finished pieces before I am fully satisfied with the outcome. This way of working is not really efficient: it takes a lot of time and concentration.

It is when I am exploring, sketching and experimenting that I think I work most efficiently and effectively. I become so absorbed by the work that my only aim at that particular time is the realisation of the object. It is not like I just sit down at my desk and make things. I need an idea first. Once an idea has presented itself to me, I work with it in my head until I begin to approach some kind of result.

At this point I undertake comprehensive research to find out whether the idea might have been used before. No matter how original our thoughts, it is always possible that some other artist has explored similar territory at some time or other before us. I spend a lot of time doing this research before taking the idea further. Originality is very important to me, not only in terms of ideas themselves, but with respect to materials and composition.

I almost never get my inspiration from existing jewellery art. This does not mean that I have lost interest in jewellery. In fact, I have a great passion for contemporary jewellery, and visit jewellery galleries and exhibitions as often as I can. I like to see the diverse concepts and uses of materials which other artists employ. Although I do not seek inspiration as such from this, nevertheless it is still an informative experience.

I tend to get my inspiration from the things around me: architecture, art, history, and from listening to music, especially music from the British jazz/rock scene.

Complete freedom, with no concern about having to sell, about production time, about delivery: this is when I am most creative and my working process is at its optimum.

At the time I made the Egg Necklace I was listening to that kind of music, especially groups from the Canterbury scene. Bands like Egg and Soft Machine made music which was completely free and very concentrated, incorporating jazz-style improvisation, rock and poetry. I think that my creative process was in many ways very similar.

For me, the egg form is one of the most perfect to be found in nature. It is fragile and beautiful. It is a symbol of time and patience. I wanted to create a construction in and on which the egg form could be presented and represented. My aim was to find a solution in which the construction could both balance and hold the egg securely while still preserving that quality of fragility.

Sigurd Bronger

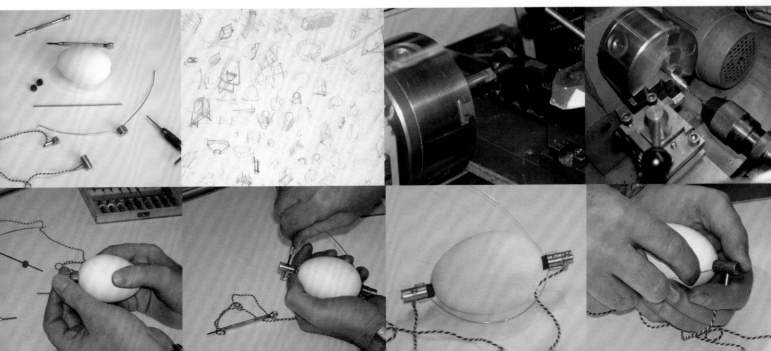

PETER CHANG

STUDIO PHILOSOPHY
One must above all maintain integrity – be true to oneself. I do not follow trends, fashion or artistic movements.

Peter Chang is one of the most interesting jewellery artists currently working. He creates sculpture and other objects as well, all activities seeming to cross-influence each other. Having originally studied graphic design, printmaking, and sculpture, he came to jewellery later and seemed at the time just to burst onto the scene with his rather novel, brightly-coloured plastic creations: serious jewellery statements intended to last, recycled from materials intended to be discarded. No one else was making work like this at that particular moment and their bold sculptural qualities were something of a shock to many of us. These at the time reminded me of South American art yet somehow had an Asian, an Eastern, feel to them too. The Liverpudlian son of a Chinese father and English mother, perhaps he and his work also exude a sense of 'the other', the exotic. A man of relatively few words, Peter tends to allow his work to speak for itself, which it does more than adequately. His statement is therefore quite short and very much to the point. The thoroughness of his approach is nevertheless manifest. He is informed by a wide range of intellectual interests which include philosophy, science, religion, and a keen interest in nature, particularly the mathematical sequences to be found therein. Most of his pieces, if they are not overtly animalistic in form, certainly have a very zoomorphic feel to them, while recent work has been described by some commentators as being futuristic, even 'Frankensteinish'.

His drawings are exploratory as well as developmental. He seems to observe and try to catch what he calls the 'essence' of nature through this activity, after a long and thorough thought process during which much of the designing is, in effect, being done. Thereafter, drawing is a developmental, refining tool, but no more than that, allowing the materials themselves to offer possibilities which might not have been obvious before. The manipulation of the materials – acrylic, polyester resin and PVC – making component parts, measuring, considering, precision cutting and fitting, are the major challenges leading to an end result that achieves a remarkable balance between intellect and intuition.

BELOW
Brooch. Acrylic, resin and gold.
10.5 x 4.5 x 2.0 cm.

OPPOSITE
Bracelet. Acrylic and resin.
11.7 x 16.8 x 6.0 cm.

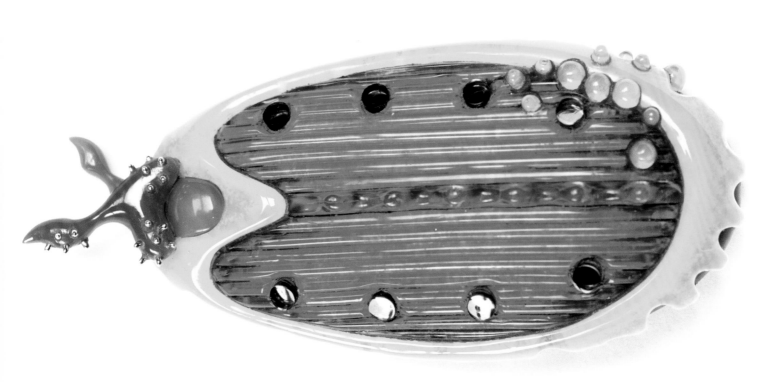

PETER CHANG

I see myself as an artist, my background training and development is that of a
sculptor and autographic printmaker.

Jewellery for me is an art-form, one of my means of self-expression within the
western tradition of the multi-facets of an artist's creative activity.

One must above all maintain integrity – be true to oneself. I do not follow trends,
fashion or artistic movements. Originality for me is achieved through honesty, what
one is born with, one's inheritance, experiences, interests and ability to express
oneself.

I try to express what is around me, my environment, my experiences, everyday
reflections of life. However, part of my exploration is also to go beyond the confines
of the western tradition, to see the world from other perspectives in order to express

ABOVE
Bracelet. Acrylic, resin and gold.
17.2 x 12.3 x 6.2 cm.

OPPOSITE
TOP ROW, LEFT TO RIGHT
Preliminary drawings are points of departure. First I cut and shape the back of the brooch in black PVC. I then cut and fit the stainless-steel pin and clasp. The form of the body of the brooch is shaped and carved out of polyurethane foam.

SECOND ROW, LEFT TO RIGHT
I then cement the back to the body and cover with GRP. I sand and smooth the GRP shape to the desired finish. Blue resin is applied.

THIRD ROW, LEFT TO RIGHT
I cut a component shape in orange acrylic. Further coats of blue resin are applied to the body, fully controlling the translucency. I sand and smooth the blue area, exposing the gradations in blue, and polish to a finish.

Thermo-form and refine the orange acrylic shape forming a 'fringe'.

FOURTH ROW, LEFT TO RIGHT
I cut an acrylic 'spine' of blue and green, form it to the desired profile and shape and polish to finish; I cut and profile the 'reeds' in green acrylic. I thermo-form and fit the reeds over the body and pigment. I cut and laminate orange acrylic sheeting, turn on a lathe to form rods of differing diameters, and cut purple acrylic mirrored shapes. The rods are cut, shaped and polished and the mirrored shapes are further cut to form rounds, the fringe is further refined to a finish.

FIFTH ROW, LEFT TO RIGHT
I assemble the fringe and reeds in position and finish rods, spine and rounds. I form 'parasitic' shapes in red and blue acrylic with gold details; cut blue acrylic connecting shape and fit to the body. I finish the connecting piece and cement all the components in situ, then polish and grout to the final finish.

new insights through my own personal vision. This research not only includes artistic activity but also philosophy, science, technology and religion.

Nature plays an important role in my work, but not to the exclusion of man-made activity in either thought or deed.

The methods of making art are not sciences and often defy logic. Like music, for me the visual arts should be approached with feeling and a balance sought between the intellect and the intuitive.

THE DEVELOPMENT OF THE BROOCH

Ideas

Ideas are all around, the problem sometimes arises in filtering out all but the strongest. In this object, what came through were thoughts and feelings about the cycle of life and nature's illustrations of parasitic and epiphytic relationships. However, I try not to literally copy but rather to grasp the 'essence' – often the abstractions can mask the original thoughts, and ambiguity plays its part. Ideas are expressed in the object itself and not in words of explanation.

Drawing

Once my ideas and directions are confirmed, I always make numerous drawings and explore a wide field of reference material, often from diverse sources, which in this case range from the plant and insect world to the bacteriological and viral manifestations found in decay. Drawings are by definition two-dimensional representations of an idea and I consider them only as 'points of departure' in preparation towards the making of a three-dimensional object.

GIOVANNI CORVAJA

STUDIO PHILOSOPHY
Talking and writing are not my strong
points: just give me a piece of gold.

BELOW AND OPPOSITE
Bracelet. 18ct gold,
20ct gold wire, black enamel.
110 x 110 x 30 mm.

Giovanni Corvaja has a very particular kind of work ethic. For him, the making is the most important part of creating. It is obvious, on reading his statement, that he has an innate ability to think an idea through thoroughly in advance, but it is his profound technical self-confidence, born out of years of steady and committed application to his craft, which allows him to take on projects of such complexity and delicacy. While many jewellers will be content to purchase ready-made or partly processed material, such as sheet metal of a given thickness, or wire already drawn down to a particular diameter by the bullion company, Giovanni will spend considerable time devising equipment which will allow him to exert total control over dimensions, finish, and quality. Everything must be as perfect as it is possible to be before he will begin what most of us would think of as the actual making: for him the preparatory work is indeed an integral part of the whole creative process.

As he indicates in his statement, if he feels that a work is not right in one way or another, even after two months of effort, he will not hesitate to melt it down and start again. I suspect that not many people would be brave enough or meticulous enough to take that decision after such intensive activity. That is a measure of his uncompromising rigour as an artist and craftsman. Having been making things since childhood, his mastery of his craft is total; consequently he thinks a job through in advance, but not by observing any set methodology. Like everyone else featured in this volume, his is an intuitive approach, even when he is planning the various jigs and specialist tools required to construct parts of the piece. He is not, however, just a miniature engineer: like others also, he believes that not only is metal being transformed from raw material into a commodity of beauty and great value, but that the creator, by virtue of effecting one transformation, is being transformed by the process as well. Such is the mystery of what we do and what it does to us.

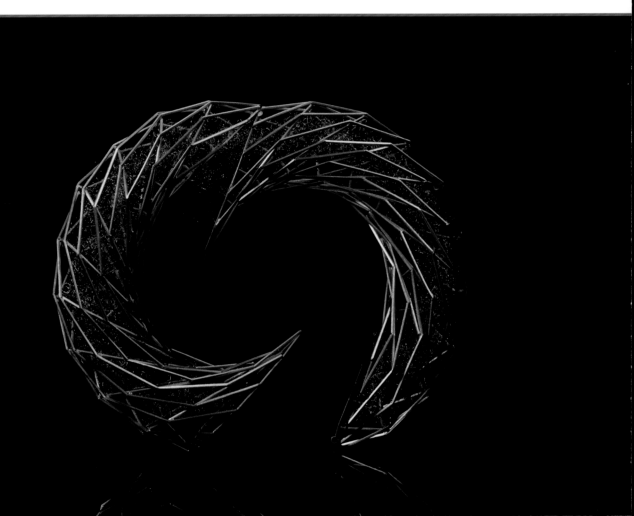

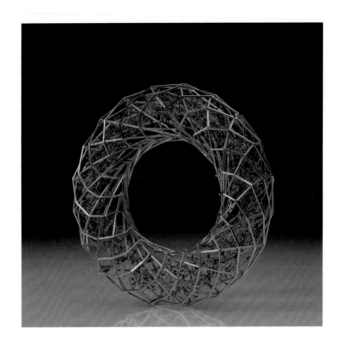

GIOVANNI CORVAJA

For me, the whole point about my jewellery is the making, so my concern is more about the work than the finished object. Finishing the object is a moment where you change from one project to another and the process is complete. A lot of people would probably say that the process is just the means to the end, but what engages me is the process and the enjoyment is more in carrying it out than in the end result.

My approach to life is to try as much as possible to live here and now and not look forward for a moment of happiness, but to enjoy every moment of the process, of the making. The achievement of working is a transformation, both of material and of ourselves. We achieve, we learn, we develop, and usually we become better. We also become more tired, but spiritually we are better. As creators, we get better, we have more knowledge, more self-knowledge and a better feel for what we do.

Creating is largely an intuitive process for me. It is quite difficult to explain my methodology because it is an acquired skill that I do not usually analyse. When you make a movement, you are not conscious of what muscles you are moving and exactly what your body is doing, you take it for granted and just do it. For this project I tried to analyse every aspect of what I did, whereas usually I just go on

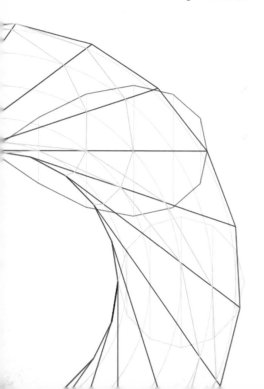

and make. For example, I can make a part that requires twenty days of labour on a milling machine and a lathe, without a single sketch, doing everything by hand, which requires me to realise the object in my mind – an ability I didn't have during the earlier years of my career; it is an acquired skill and older craftsmen probably have it much more than me. This process changes the material – in this case gold – but it also changes us. Makers are material as much as the gold.

For me, drawing is like making jewellery or sculpture. It is a form of expression and I find it extremely important when you communicate an idea of what the object will look like long before actually creating it. When I teach, for example, I get very frustrated if my students don't know how to draw, because they cannot present what they have in their mind and communicate it to me. I have to assess the idea and think of the technical solution. Of course, a drawing can be a form of expression in itself, as in the case of an illustrator or a painter. For the bracelet illustrated here, the drawing was essential for determining the section and how that would be constructed – something I could not just do mentally. I needed a technical drawing, which six months before I would have done on a sheet of paper, to determine all those teardrop shapes precisely. Every angle, whether you do it graphically or using a computer with a CAD programme, is critical; otherwise it is not very clear how you make the basic shape that determines the elements that become the main skeleton of the piece. In this case, CAD saved me a day of technical drawing.

I have always preferred to work from first principles. I drew down the gold wire very carefully to the finest diameter appropriate to the job in hand. Even if I could buy wire of such small diameter, it would not have the refined quality I require, nor would it offer the making experience which is of paramount importance to me. Similarly, I could not find good quality enamel in chunks, so I melted powdered enamel in a gold foil and made a solid mass from which I then formed strands, and these strands I fused into the tiny cell-like forms using a lampwork technique similar to that used by the glassworkers on the Venetian island of Murano.

The brass die took several days to make, but it allowed me to solder together all the gold parts with total accuracy, without them moving because of the heat. I always try to be as careful and as precise as possible. I am convinced that one mistake leads to another; you can never fully compensate for those mistakes, as they simply add to each other and make more problems for you. So, it is imperative to always try to be precise.

I do not want to see something that is not right. I recently worked for two months on a piece that I felt was not right, so I re-melted it and started again. There are some moments when you just have to start again. You have actually already

achieved something by starting again, because it is not only the transformation of the material but also the transformation of you. So, if after two months you know it is not right, you are a better person. By doing that you are removing a burden from your life. Of course, some accidents can happen in a moment of tiredness, or a wrong movement can ruin a piece. I always think that we should put all our effort into what we do, but after all, it is only jewellery. We are not doctors; it is not someone's body that we might have damaged, so a mistake is not such a disaster. We are doing things that are new: new for us, and sometimes for other people, so mistakes can happen.

Fear of making a mistake is usually the first cause of the mistake itself, because you try too hard to be careful, but you have to be relaxed, don't tense your muscles, you should have a good and healthy approach to what you are doing.

To me, working with gold is like playing a musical instrument. Technically, the physics of it is quite straightforward and simple; the high level of skill is something you acquire with a lot of discipline. I consider myself lucky that I started this training when I was a young teenager; I was thirteen years old and even as a child, before attending technical art school, I always worked with my hands, so I had a disposition for precise manual work. If people start when they are eighteen or nineteen, I think it is more difficult, and therefore more work and more time are required to achieve any level of mastery.

I believe that it takes ten years to achieve mastery of the craft, depending on how intensively you work. I considered myself a goldsmith about ten or twelve years after starting, when I was in my late twenties. I think that we are always developing and improving. I also think that our profession needs a number of skills, so to master them all properly you need to learn more than for many other jobs.

My hands are my main organ of expression. Verbalising or writing about my thoughts is one thing, but materialising them with my hands is more normal. This is why I find it difficult to write or even talk about what I do and how I do it. I am perfectly able to demonstrate what I do, but talking and writing are not my strong points: just give me a piece of gold.

BRACELET, 2011

I like it when beauty is discovered bit by bit, slowly, by careful observation. Often beauty is hidden by its size.

The bracelet is composed of a frame in 18ct red gold holding and containing a fine mist of 20ct gold wires that suspends many small shapes of black enamel.

The images show the finished object before the making process, because that is how people (the public) usually approach an object.

The enamel elements are worked as 'micro lamp-work'. To do this, I had to melt the powdered enamel into a small ingot. I therefore made a small tray in pure gold to hold the enamel while it was melting in the kiln, which peeled off the enamel when it became solid. By heating pieces of enamel until it became soft and extendible, I made several wires from it. One by one I made the tiny black elements by sinking the thin gold thread into the melted enamel, working in front of a microflame. Each wire section is approximately 150 mm in length and holds at each end one enamel shape.

The 'cage' is a round toroid, sliced diagonally, divided into two sections and hinged. It is made of 18ct gold wire, with a hexagonal section. To hold the twenty sections in the right position while soldering the whole structure, I turned a bronze tool with slots at the correct angle and soldered the frame at as many points as possible before removing everything from the tool and finishing the soldering. I finished the surface of the structure with a very sharp and highly polished scraper.

I then attached the thin wires to the frame with a simple knot.

Giovanni Corvaja

ABOVE
Bracelet detail.
18ct gold, 20ct gold wire,
black enamel.
110 x 110 x 30 mm.

SIMON COTTRELL

STUDIO PHILOSOPHY
My work doesn't aim to tell a viewer anything; and for myself I simply enjoy the act of devising tangible form from insights into intangible phenomena.

BELOW
"Tagged tubed bod" brooch. Monel, stainless steel. 75 x 40 x 30 mm.

Simon Cottrell is emphatic in stating that he does not use drawing at all as a creative medium. Reading his statement, it becomes quite clear that he is well read and informed. His is an ongoing journey of open-minded enquiry. He insists that his works are not designed in any formal sense but that they evolve from a largely intuitive process. He can think and 'see' in three dimensions, and apparently just gets on with making. As I understand it, he creates through a structured form of improvisation in much the same way that a jazz musician develops an initial theme and, through a complex combination of prior knowledge, experience, and intuition, eventually reaches a final destination, having along the way visited other places too. He is content to take his time as he recognises the changes and developments taking place in a piece or collection of pieces, and allows himself to gradually work through these as they present themselves. For him the many, complex parts of the journey are certainly as intriguing and valuable as the destination. A number of our artists refer to how ongoing projects influence each other, how themes (visual and subjective) present themselves over a period of years and sometimes will repeat themselves in different forms from one project to another. For Simon this is a deliberate approach, each brooch developing out of the previous one, sometimes several being in a state of more or less simultaneous creation. He has a particular interest in what he calls 'sensory attentiveness and perception' as a factor in creativity. I take this to mean not quite the actual making and the specific feel of the materials, but how what he thinks of as his acute perception of each stage in a project informs and influences the next in that ongoing series of mental and physical, conscious and subconscious, decision-makings-in-action.

He expresses a particular concern about the cognitive process in craft practice and eloquently articulates the need for craftspeople to be more aware and enquiring of how and why we do what we do.

SIMON COTTRELL

I have always been intrigued by the innate and fundamental nature of things –
how and why things happen – and I have always had an attentive eye for pattern
recognition within human behaviour (my own and that of others). So it is no great
surprise that my 'creative' pursuits have developed in a way that is stimulated and
informed by insights into the broad phenomenology of creative process and all
the underlying processes within human nature that facilitate its actions. My work
(predominantly fixated on brooches at present) is not 'designed' in a formal sense,
instead they're intuitive pieces, and hence each one starts from the awareness and
memory of all previous works. I just sit down and start making, while watching very
closely over my own shoulder.

While there is a seemingly strict set of 'parameters' that define many aspects of
the way I work, these parameters also slowly progress by intuitive evolution. Once
an outcome of an intuitive action is cognitively judged as a positive progression,
it is then consciously added to these 'parameters'. These parameters are born of
a reflexive process, some aspects of which (like choice of material and tectonics)

have barely shifted in well over a decade. The manner through which I build forms with interleaving planes began as a means of making simple forms with complex definition. This process I have almost exhausted and I am using less and less. I don't seem to be interested in fast movement, but prefer to explore thoroughly and pedantically all that I see as having any potential. So, rather than simply jumping in different directions to entirely new aims and approaches, I'm more inclined to progress slowly from one idea to another. This is because paying close attention to the paths towards points of transition, between certain ideas/qualities/sensations, can reveal far more than what is present at the origin or destination itself.

For the aims of this book it is not really possible to separate an artist's statement from an explanation of my creative process, as the two are so thoroughly intertwined. Explaining the manner of creative progression in my work is not best done by looking at the making of one individual piece of jewellery. Much of the progress that best illustrates my creative priorities is more evident over a longer period of time by looking 'between' pieces. I have often referred to all my work as one large piece, simply because in essence it all shares the very same aim. This is best described as 'a personal rightness', even though exactly what constitutes this aim is always in a steady state of progressive flow also.

This image of two pieces (below) illustrates something of the nature of this flow. The piece on the left was made in 2002 for an exhibition. A few months later, during that exhibition, I was asked to submit the same piece for another exhibition in another country. Considering the simplicity of the piece, I decided to make a second one. The new piece was made with the basic structure of the first in mind while

BELOW
"Three drops one gold ONE" and "Three drops one gold TWO" brooches. Monel, 666 gold, stainless steel. 40 x 50 x 25 mm (each).

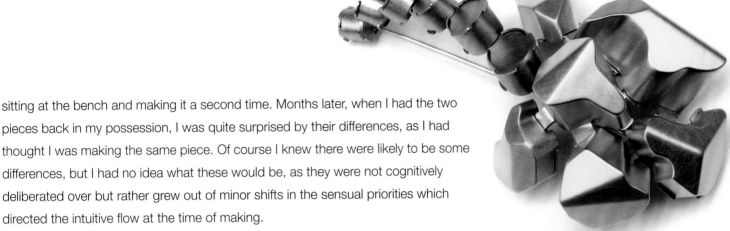

sitting at the bench and making it a second time. Months later, when I had the two pieces back in my possession, I was quite surprised by their differences, as I had thought I was making the same piece. Of course I knew there were likely to be some differences, but I had no idea what these would be, as they were not cognitively deliberated over but rather grew out of minor shifts in the sensual priorities which directed the intuitive flow at the time of making.

This occurrence really sparked my interest into the progression of creative process (and all processes that constitute it) rather than the end outcomes alone. Most of the time, the manner of this flow is more of a subconscious reductive process – a refinement of what has been done before – rather than consciously drawing on new things from outside. However, outcomes of intuitive play that I later deem as positives are often consciously absorbed into these parameters also.

More recently I've been looking at the role of sensory attentiveness and perception within the processes of intuitive creativity. It is sensory attentiveness that gives us deeper understanding of 'cause and effect' and their importance in the continued development and progress of idea/concept and also in relation to physical manual engagement and material control. The piece 'blob, faceted tubes progression' 2006 is an example where the form of the piece grows and develops much as an idea starts simply and then complicates itself in a variety of directions.

With 'Bang in/at plant' 2007 and most works between 2007 and 2009 I have looked at how we are hard-wired to attempt to make clear sense of new experiences, and proceeded to make work that utilised this fact as a means to extend perceptual processes. When our senses are presented with something that is familiar and yet also ambiguous, our curiosity is triggered and sensory engagement is extended. This is because our ability to be definitive about what we are actually looking at struggles to reach a clear resolve.

If there is a potential line between these objects being perceived in one way or another, I will try to sit on that line. Where that line lies, however, depends very much on the attentiveness of the viewer. Hence the ambiguity here is multi-layered and often in a state of flux. Are these pieces serious or playful? Complex or simple? Monotonous or dynamic? Plants or anatomy? Rocks or clouds? Flowers or exploding ammunition? I am building structures, details and relationships between

ABOVE
"Village of gold teeth with tail" brooch. Monel, gold-plated monel, stainless steel. 105 x 55 x 40 mm.

BELOW
"Tight/open mixed cluster bang" brooch. Monel, 666 gold, stainless steel. 55 x 65 x 35 mm.

ABOVE
"Six tall dimples from/
through/behind" brooch.
Monel, stainless steel.
85 x 55 x 40 mm.

them that have the potential to be all of the above and many more things beyond.

I want to be clear that I do not often sit down with conscious aims as to how I'm going build this ambiguity. I often start with one shape and then add another in response to it, and then another in response to relationships between the previous two, and so on. If at any point along this path I notice that the growing structure is starting to evoke a particular subject, I will actively continue in a way that further develops that subject while at the same time adding forms, details and structure that contradict that subject. Often, this process evokes entirely new subjects, so once again I both reinforce and contradict these also. The fact that my brooches are over the years becoming ever more voluminous is a direct result of this reflexive and progressive process. This volume of the forms also allows for more drastic shifts in perception, depending on the angles from which the brooch is viewed. Here I am talking about both the way I view them as they are being made and also how the wearer will view the finished piece.

Over the last year I have been making work that looks more specifically at the nature of creative progression, not so much within the development and making of one piece, but over several years. The piece 'bulbs to barn doors' combines much of the progress over the previous three years and 'round and back in tempers' covers the last six years. With these pieces the parameters are quite simply a starting point and an end point. All that happens between this is left to intuitive flow.

I have only discussed briefly a few of the processes I'm toying with in my work. I do not have the space to delve into all of them here and now. Not a single aspect has been left as incidental. With insights into the multi-layered and predominantly subconscious processes and how they work and inter-relate, I find that it is possible to intervene and more clearly facilitate the increasingly complex parameters and the way the direct intuitive progression moves.

All subconscious action has a starting point within some kind of set parameters. Even where artists have little awareness of these processes, intuition is subconsciously working within certain parameters, often quite simply set by the artist's underlying priorities of personal 'taste', which direct their conscious (and subconscious) actions without them even being aware of their influence.

I have had people suggest to me that my approach, which in effect is consciously applying what was once left to the realm of the subconscious, is a limitation to the freedom that should be at the basis of the phenomenon that is creative process. A solid counterpoint to this simplistic view is expressed here by Rudolf Arnheim:[1]

A common prejudice has it that verbal analysis (of creative process) paralyses intuitive creation and comprehension ... But are we to conclude that in the arts one power of the mind must be suspended so that another may function? Is it not true that disturbances occur precisely when any one faculty operates at the expense of another? The delicate balance of all a person's powers – which alone permits one to live fully and to work well – is potentially upset not only when the intellect interferes with intuition, but also when sensation dislodges reasoning. Groping in vagueness is no more productive than blind adherence to rules. Unchecked self-analysis can be harmful, but not as much as the artificial primitivism of the person who refuses to understand the innate fundamentals of how and why they work.

BELOW LEFT
"Bang in/at plant" brooch.
Monel, black powder-coat,
stainless steel.
70 x 60 x 40 mm.

BELOW RIGHT
"Variable Focus" brooch.
Monel blackened, stainless
steel. 45 x 55 x 40 mm.

I do not believe that any degree of analysis can change the nature of any phenomena. All my analysis does is define more clearly the processes through which I direct the cognitive parameters that act as foundations from which intuitive creative phenomena work. This view is more succinctly explained below.[2]

No serious empirical researcher and no philosopher want to 'reduce consciousness'; at best, one theory about how the contents of conscious experience arose can be reduced to another theory. Our theories about phenomena change, but the phenomena stay the same. A beautiful rainbow continues to be a beautiful rainbow even after it has been explained in terms of electromagnetic radiation...

As Metzinger suggests, even if the theories I use to enlighten myself to my own actions never offer anything other than further questions and indefinite open-ended answers, surely this is more valuable than never having enquired in the first place? It could also be argued that using the brain to understand the brain itself is bound to be fraught with troubles, so I feel that shedding light on these subjects clarifies and resolves the ways and means by which my cognitive aims are brought into being through intuitive processes

Why do all this within jewellery? ... Well, why not? Personal creative process (or more generally, developmental forward progression) is a fundamental part of human nature and also the basis of the manner through which we learn anything. What I am mindfully doing within this creative work, I am already subconsciously doing within everything else that I do. The human body itself is the vehicle that builds the bridge between an idea and its tangible iteration; what better place to site the outcomes of such a process?

In essence, my work doesn't aim to tell a viewer anything; and for myself I simply enjoy the act of devising tangible form from insights into intangible phenomena. My primary influences are not visual, but I do want to give the wearer and the viewer a personal sensory experience, in a lasting, resonant, but quiet manner. No matter how closely we look ... or the angle from which

BELOW
"Hollow lumps with white tubes" brooch. Monel, stainless steel, enamel paint. 70 x 50 x 30 mm.

we view them ... on what clothes or in which way we wear them, all these pieces are not conceived to be made clear sense of. Rather, the aim is to offer a gentle shifting diversity of perceptual readings depending on the context of the viewing. The more you look, the more you see. The more you see, the more the relationships between your perceptions of certain details begin to progress and change. Through this your cognitive building of links between sensual stimulus and applied meaning also begins to shift and change. There can be no punch line in this work, although it is inevitable that your mind will attempt to find one.

Simon Cottrell

ABOVE
"Bulbs to barn doors"
brooch. Monel, stainless
steel. 70 x 50 x 30 mm.

NOTES

1. Rudolf Arnheim, *Art and Visual Perception: A Psychology of the Creative Eye* (50th anniversary edition), 2004

2. Thomas Metzinger. *The Ego Tunnel: The Science of the Mind and the Myth of the Self*. Basic Books, 2009

RAMON PUIG CUYÀS

STUDIO PHILOSOPHY
Creating is my way of satisfying
an indefinable need to transform,
construct, illuminate.

BELOW AND OPPOSITE
Preparatory sketches and work
in progress: Nº 1338. Brooch.
Net-Work Series. Nickel silver.
60 x 85 x 22 mm.

Ramon Puig Cuyàs is another jeweller whose work is founded in a surefooted (perhaps I should say surehanded) technique. He seems to have a demonstrable confidence in being able to make up any of his ideas, and talks about this quite matter-of-factly. For him, making is all part of thinking. I am certain that is shared with all the others in this volume and is, I believe, another demonstration of that haptic sensibility which makes one think of the hand as an extended part of the brain. He talks about creating himself through making, not just creating a work of art. This is transformation not just of materials and ideas but of oneself through the creative process, something which other jewellery artists describe too. He refers also to an element of pre-knowledge, that store of tacit knowledge which we all build up over a period of years, often without fully realising what we have until somehow or other the ideas just seem to rise to the surface and begin to manifest themselves: on paper, in card, in metals, or other materials which we find on the bench or in drawers, bags, wallets, or suitcases.

Ramon also makes interesting musical analogies, referring to harmonies, polyphony, tempo and equilibrium, reminding me somewhat of how Richard Sennett talks about some of the qualities of craftsmanship. In spite of, or perhaps because of, these analogies, his work is intensely metaphorical. It is indefinably ambiguous in many ways too. Drawing for him is a means of exploring new ideas and their many variations, but he is quite clear that it is when he is working directly with his chosen materials that the experience and activity is at its most intense. He is clear about how each piece is the result of continuous experimentation, of trying out different possibilities, juxtapositions, relationships, and thereby attempting to realise and visually describe 'an expression of consciousness'.

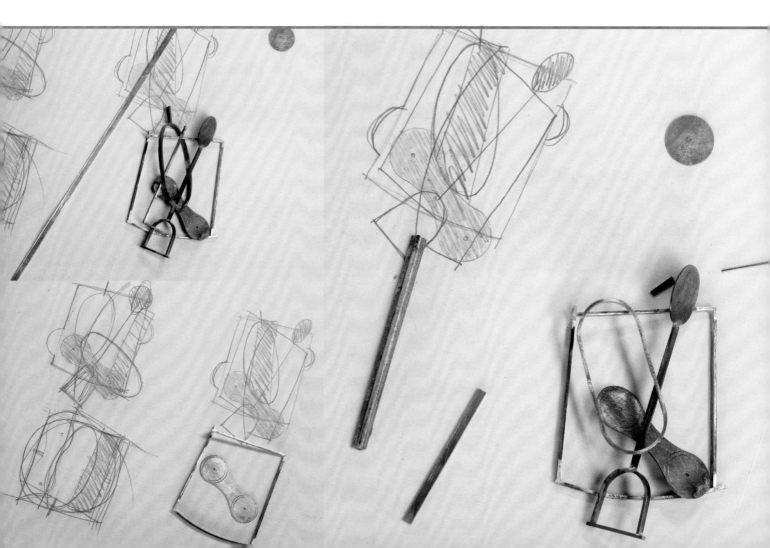

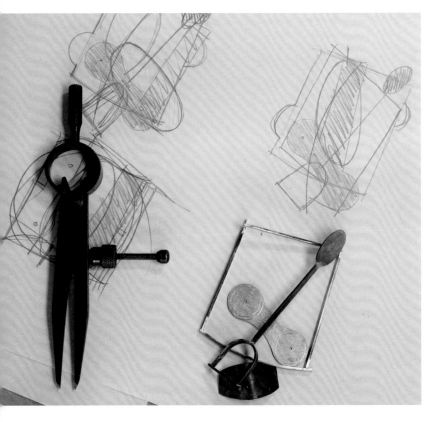

RAMON
PUIG CUYÀS

The activity of creating is an adventure which takes me away from the everyday, casting me beyond horizons of known and assured things. It doesn't matter what medium we employ, whether it be jewellery or painting, music or writing, to create is to invent oneself, to create oneself.

Creating is my way of satisfying an indefinable need to transform, construct, illuminate, to turn the invisible into the visible and to be able to do so with my own hands. The act of creation is like a journey to conquer an innermost sense of freedom, and to satisfy a deep desire to feel myself alive. I am impelled to commence each new work by the need to respond to a challenge, that of turning a pre-feeling into a real feeling. Planning and constructing is to live the experience of some moments of tidiness and emotion.

Each piece of jewellery emerges after a long process wrought from repetition, rehearsal, elimination, selection and decision, as well as an evolution of feelings, emotions, certainties and doubts. This process is an attempt to reveal, to materialise something indefinable, such as an internal design born of intuition, in order to turn it into an expression of consciousness.

Although I start each new work without any plan or prior schema, my most recent finished piece often stands as a model for me to use and so realise what I must look for next. Whilst drawing and making exploratory sketches, I attempt to go into a state of concentration, of active attention, in order to listen, feel or provoke an internal pre-vision. I search for a mental image which serves as a guide, though nothing is defined or specific. The drawings frequently serve to explore new paths and variations in composition, although it is when working directly with the materials that the dialogue becomes more intense.

Both experience and technical mastery facilitate a handling of materials, tools and hands with apparent ease, enabling their expression. I endeavour deliberately to leave in those traces and marks made through the working process, as they are the records of this dialogue. Working with my hands awakens in me a sense of humanity; it makes me more perceptive and sharpens the senses. Thought and clarity are almost always arrived at through action, they come with that dialogue between materials and shapes. Making is for me a way of thinking, and I try to ensure that the result of this making is a testament, materialised through a piece of jewellery charged with the will to express.

BELOW, LEFT TO RIGHT:
Preparatory sketches and
work in progress: Nº 1344.
Pendant. Net-Work Series.
Nickel silver.
40 x 25 x 120 mm.

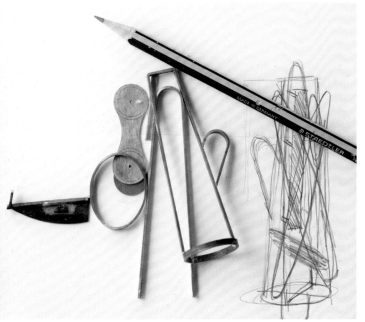
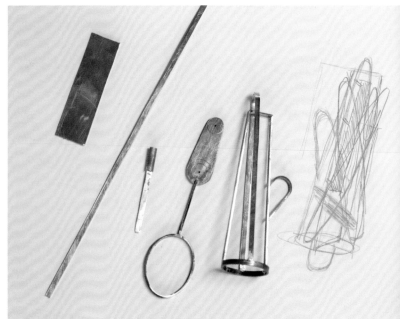

I like to improvise when in contact with the materials, exploring their possibilities and stretching their limits. Working with a material allows me to assess results immediately and in a direct way. I attempt to make the process of creation one of flow rather than fight, such that solutions appear naturally, as though inevitable. However, at times the best results appear only after hard and persistent effort.

Formally, I need to structure my pieces on the basis of a strict compositional syntax which either comes close to, or gives the impression of, polyphony. I seek a sound, or harmonies amongst the straight and curved lines, in the variations of planes and in the contrasts amid colours and materials. I try to create an order whereby the chaos of ideas and feelings reigns.

It is possibly for this reason that most of my works are structured compositionally as separate elements, as assemblies, thereby creating virtual spaces rather than filled volume. I ensure that the object as a whole isn't seen, not completely perceived at first sight. Instead, the gaze wanders and runs around a subtle network of visual itineraries, exploring and discovering harmonious and contrasting relationships amongst the various parts of the object, making a necessary tempo for the gaze to linger on, staying in every corner of the overall composition. In this way the viewer's gaze isn't passive, rather it is participative.

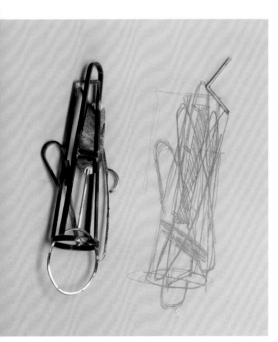

OPPOSITE
Nº 1344. Pendant.
Net-Work Series.
Nickel silver.
40 x 25 x 120 mm.

BELOW
Nº 1361. Brooch.
Net-Work Series.
Nickel silver.

For me, this sought compositional harmony is like a metaphor for the desire – the need – to reconstruct the harmony and equilibrium between man and nature. Making a piece of jewellery is to illuminate a microcosm that must take part in the balance and harmony of the macrocosm.

Colour has been a fundamental element in my work for many years, both part of my nature and my cultural and everyday surroundings. Colour gives me the opportunity to accentuate the expressive qualities of the composition.

Yet not all is harmony and balance, as tension and conflict are fundamental too for the act of creation to be fertile. Tensions and a conflict of feelings were the framework around which I worked to make the series Imago Mundi and Utopos, between 2007 and 2010. Something that was there already suddenly emerged unexpectedly, giving a fresh thrust to creative strengths. Colour disappeared, black and white with some grey tinges were then sufficient to stir up a much denser atmosphere in comparison with previous works. Black and white, shapes and materials, microcosms and macrocosms, all these established a suggestive dialectic, laden with meaning.

Everything, whether lines, planes, volume, textures, materials, colours, the technique employed, the very composition, all these elements become metaphor. Nothing should be gratuitous, everything has to be filled with meaning and the best method I know of to achieve this is through visual metaphor. The metaphor is a carrier for ideas, while I also like it because it does so in an ambiguous and imprecise way. It suggests symmetries and contrasts, it sets up subtle analogies, it contains implicit potential. The metaphor charges the piece of jewellery with various meanings, although it cannot, nor would it want to, explain these meanings conceptually. It is precisely because of this lack of definition that the metaphor helps me to materialise in images all that pertains to the world of the non-definable, which tends to be much more interesting than the rational and definable world.

Finally then, my work's central aim is for the object produced by my hands to be more than just a form of expression, rather it should be a way of sharing with others the experience lived through my working process, of all that I've found, discovered and made visible. And also to suggest to the wearer that the simple gesture of putting on a piece of jewellery can in itself also become a metaphor.

Ramon Puig Cuyàs

Translation: Anne Michie

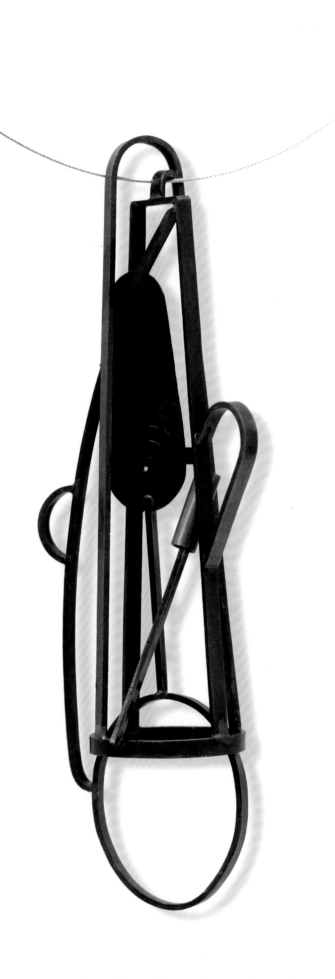

TOP ROW, LEFT TO RIGHT
Knitted wool, wool with hair,
gold-plated copper, tree bark,
breast plate, pearl chain with
gold, sculpey, flattened bird,
Michigan flowers, sandblasted
copper plate, pantyhose, gold,
pearls, leather, oval, veneer,
cuttlefish, silver and porcelain.
Hand chains, bark, birds
in cages, hair of three
generations, hanging breasts.
Flattened bird in cage.
Breast plate, pearl chain, aging
hair, flowers, ovals and trees.
Price tags and lumps of flesh.

So how do I work? I collect things, pile them up, listen to them talk to one another, striking up conversations. I introduce strangers to each other, urge them to meet, giving them a space in which to get to know each other. I rearrange them, and change the direction of their conversations. I collect and order, trying to find the key to what is hidden in objects and materials. I surround myself with things that trigger and provoke me.

I sense a narrative and I make it up while working. I could say that I try to sharpen a blurry picture; I work my way towards something that only comes into being because I sense its existence. I am not loyal to my hidden stories: they serve me as crutches, but as soon as I can walk I leave them behind, and I observe the battle of my narrative and the materials I wove into it.

I push an imaginary frontier. The many works-in-progress on my table behave like an ants' nest: the materials keep moving and shifting until they fall into their slots. This is not a peaceful process, but a good battle maintaining itself at its highest peak, refusing to let the tension subside. The intermingling of technique and culture, high and low, familiar and strange, moves the work away from legible terrains to a space that does not immediately resonate with what went into its making. I lose

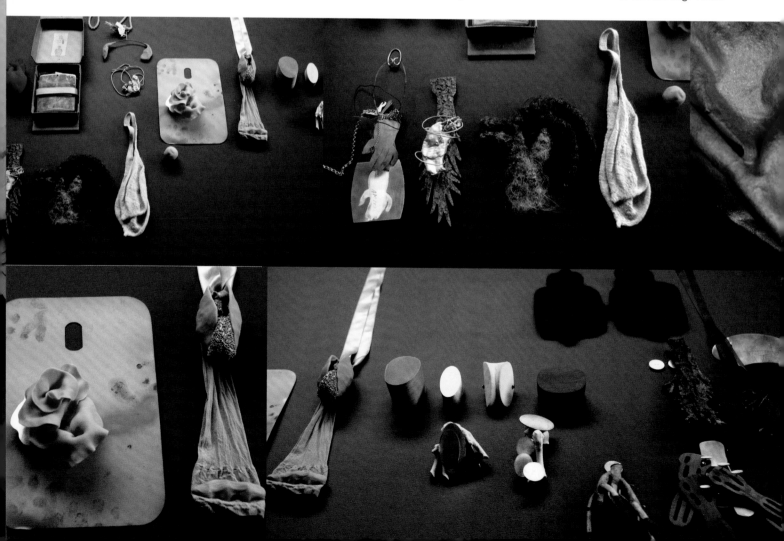

myself in time-consuming labour, not aiming for efficiency, but investing in ostensible nothingness.

Fusing and melting the ugly and the beautiful, merging the seductive and the repulsive, just to reach the moment of what is, after all, a form of beauty, a beauty that challenges, that may not be pleasing, but that offers the comfort of an ongoing endeavour.

Making use of contradictions to create friction and to convey an internal dialogue in each piece of work is what I will end up doing and making again. Playing with the viewer's expectations, but never fulfilling them. I never work on one piece only – there is always a group, each member of which is helping the other to become.

To evoke sensation with an object, in a form that barely exists: even if you cannot put your finger on its beauty, you keep wondering why, being so contracted and introverted, it is yet so beautiful. I can realise and recognise this beauty in found objects, objects that are produced by coincidence or accidents, left behind, unnoticed. They sit on my table as models of what I am aiming for, but can never reach. I see and hear the former owners of objects, but I cannot talk to them.

BOTTOM ROW, LEFT TO RIGHT
Fingerprints and clutching.
Chatelaines, necklaces and brooches.
Tenements and timelines.
Found objects, given objects, ex votos, painting behind glass and ears.
Kitchen tools and spitting images.
Time frames and bones.

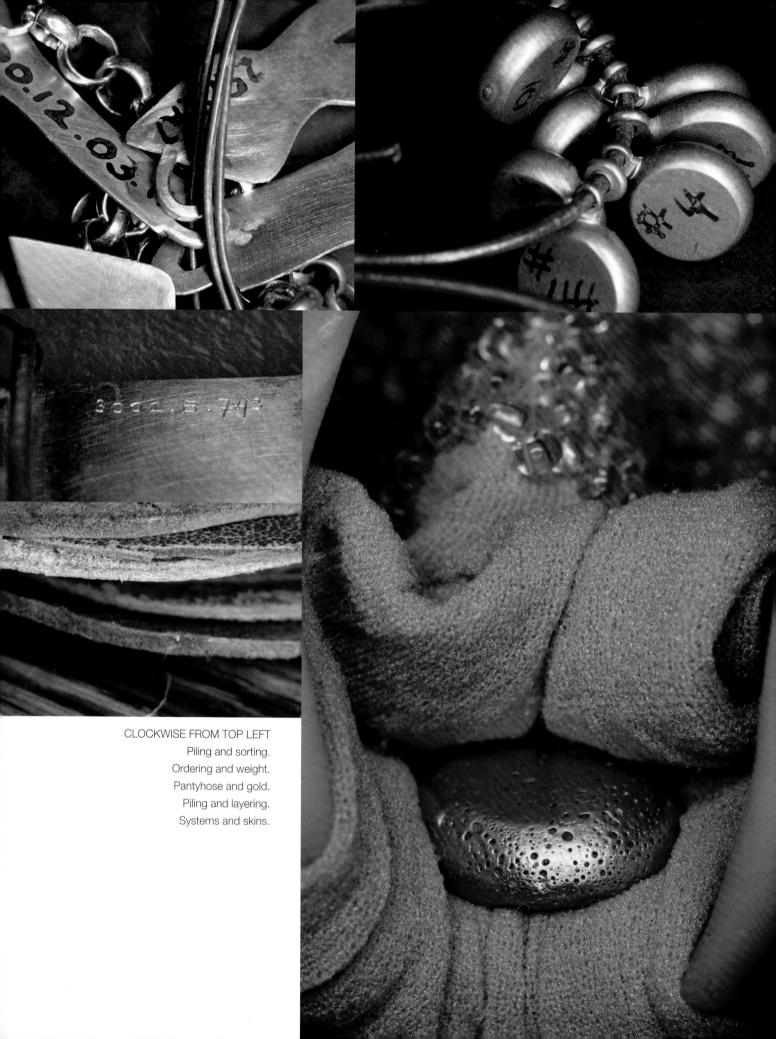

CLOCKWISE FROM TOP LEFT
Piling and sorting.
Ordering and weight.
Pantyhose and gold.
Piling and layering.
Systems and skins.

I am not scared of old-fashioned solutions or forbidden combinations. Turning the everyday, the ordinary into something precious. The rituals of using run parallel to the rituals of making.

So, what do I see when I revisit/reconfigure my work of the past twenty years? What are the recurring themes and subjects? How do I order? It seems that, however hard I try to distance myself from a subject, it will present itself again and again. Interrelated numbers and branches keep suggesting hidden systems. I use the representation of Nature as a larger system in which to get lost. I use connections, periods, seasons as a way to accept the coming and going.

Surfaces and structures, colours always mimicking or sensing the body and its outer layers. Even if ovals remain empty, there is always the suggestion of a being/a portrait. The absence of the object, or the remnants of a process: both are ways of talking about longing for the presence of a person or the landscape of ourselves. The portrait in its absence is a re-emerging image of loss and love.

It seems that I rarely introduce colour into my work, and only use it if I need to evoke a certain period or moment in time, and if I know for certain that it will not be 'nice'. Niceness is a stage to overcome, a making room for a pleasurable stroke against the grain.

As much as I feel attracted to beautiful craftsmanship, there is a line that I will not cross. This may explain why there are no drawings, no testing of techniques, no traceable map to expose and demonstrate the process of making. My work is the drawing of itself by itself, and it always retains the quality of a fast drawing, no matter how long I worked on it.

Iris Eichenberg

BELOW, LEFT TO RIGHT
Looking backwards, reflection, ovals and kitchens.
Empty pages, hands and funnels, voluptuous volumes, silver and lace.
Signatures, cleanliness and remnants.

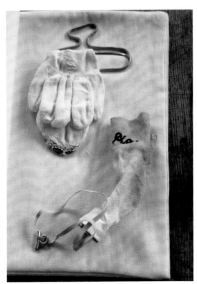

YOKO IZAWA

STUDIO PHILOSOPHY
I feel more comfortable leaving things open to interpretation or, in other words, ambiguous

BELOW
Each work starts with a single thread, part trace connecting with past ideas, part filament between new points to be marked in three-dimensional space.

OPPOSITE
Colours are inspired by my memories of Japanese natural and cultivated scenery.

Yoko Izawa came to study jewellery in the UK after several years working as a packaging designer in her native Japan. She makes it very clear that, although it may well have been unintentional, her cultural and professional background has had a profound impact on her jewellery practice. She became acutely aware of her cultural difference as a student but, rather than being overwhelmed by that – as could have happened – she turned it to her advantage. Those of us who have travelled in the East, especially in Japan, may well have been confused at times by a national reserve, perfect manners, an apparent lack of enthusiasm or of strong reaction, an ambiguity in the social context. So Yoko has, as a result of her own experience of international social disjunction, in some ways embodied that ambiguity in her work. She has used her own personality trait of avoiding defining things as a creative tool. It is almost as if, as she became more attuned to Western society and *mores*, her jewellery came to quite specifically embody qualities of reserve, mystery, and 'distance'. There is an inscrutability about her pieces, setting up a series of questions and an (often) unspoken dialogue around the space within, the unseen, the unseeable. Japanese philosophy and spirituality are implicit in Yoko's work and her way of creating seems to have a sense of this too. Drawing is part of the process, but it is the use of the materials, the working of the mechanical knitting machine, how it feels, that really inform the development and the final forms she realises. The experience of holding the 'stocking' in the hand, how it reacts by stretching and contracting, offers clues for direction and conclusion, while still shrouding the inner forms and hiding them from discovery by either wearer or onlooker.

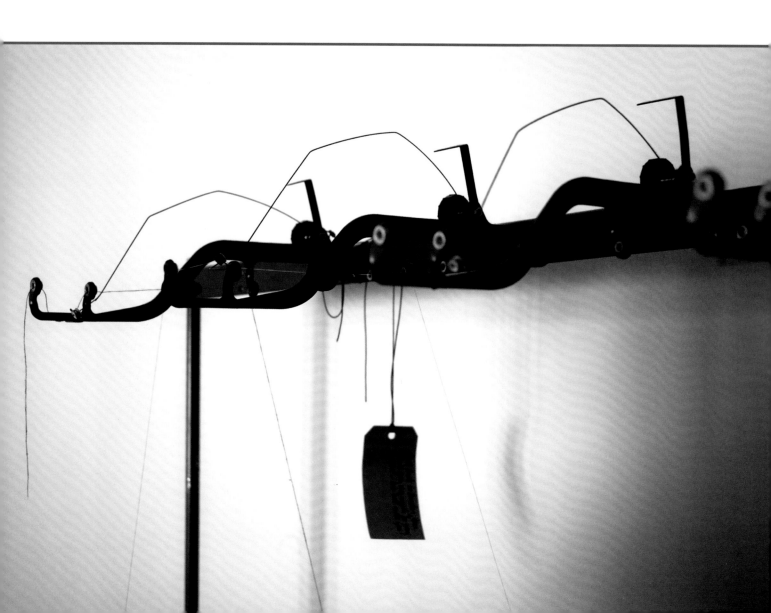

YOKO IZAWA

VEILED

Living in a different culture always makes us consider more deeply where we are from. In 1998, after seven years of practice as a packaging designer, I left Japan and came to the UK for further study. While I was a student at Kent Institute of Art and Design, I began to be aware of some significant differences in my creative expression from other students in the way I created forms and in the way I treated materials. While at the Royal College of Art, these questions made me further explore my inner self to find out what kind of sense of values and aesthetics I had, and subsequently made me realise how much I was influenced by Japanese culture. What I discovered about myself was that I always try to avoid defining things. This is almost instinctive. I tend to choose something in between two opposed features: neither 'yes' nor 'no', 'black' nor 'white', or could be both. I feel more comfortable leaving things open to interpretation or, in other words, ambiguous. Actually, this ambiguity is the quintessence of Japanese culture and can be traced back even to our religious spirituality, which is animistic and polytheistic.

Synchronising to these processes of contemplation of myself and my cultural background, I started to search for some ways to express – in three-dimensional scale – my very own language.

ABOVE FROM LEFT
Investigation of tactile properties in the tensions between an inner structure and an outer skin. Drawings explore not edges or forms, but rather the essence of a vessel that might capture the spirit of a 'void'.
The notion of nothingness is realised through light captured in an empty volume.

OPPOSITE, TOP
"Petal" necklace.

OPPOSITE, BOTTOM
"Inro" rings, conveying voids. Inro is the name for the traditional container worn with kimonos for carrying small precious objects, and these 'jewels' contain my ideas about Japanese notions of space.

A eureka moment happened when I was working with amber, which I hadn't particularly liked. I intuitively covered it with my snagged stocking. The result was something more than I expected. I found a synergy between inside and outside materials such that all the elements such as form, texture, colour, weight and tension visually merged into one. The harshness of amber was softened by this delicate and transparent skin-like material, and only its beauty was brought up to the surface. Also the whole object looked rather animated by being given a skin and body. Above all, what made me most excited about this new object was that it had an ambiguous quality in which one could perceive opposing features simultaneously: inside and outside, rigid and flexible, strength and delicacy, as well as hidden and visible.

This is how my 'Veiled' series of jewellery started. Soon afterwards I discovered the way to produce this fine elastic knitting myself. It is now a signature of my work, and a tool that gives me an opportunity to further investigate these 'veiled' objects. Since then I have been concentrating on exploring the possibilities within this unique combination.

Since I am always fascinated by ambiguous expressions, to investigate what is underneath this attitude has been my main research interest. As I mentioned, this is definitely related to Japanese culture. Each culture has its own core or foundation on which it has been built, but, in the case of Japan, the core itself seems something indescribable and ambiguous, yet still perceivable.

It is said that the central concept in our Eastern thoughts is 'nothingness', but this is not about a nothingness or emptiness in quantity or quality, something which we can measure or compare. 'Nothingness' can be imagined as the condition before things emerged or the condition before things were divided.[1] Nothingness can be described as infinite and alive with possibility.[2]

OPPOSITE
"Dew Drops" necklace.

'Things are either devolving toward, or evolving from, nothingness. The universe is in constant motion toward or away from potential.'[3]

This explains well how I feel or understand the world I belong to, and what we call 'life'. In this way of thinking, aesthetically, impermanence or transience becomes appreciated and celebrated.

Another core idea in Japanese culture which I sense in my work is depth, or as we say, 'oku'.[4] This is not about actual measurable depth, but a sense of depth or sense of centre which you feel in your mind, in another word, profoundness. In Japanese culture, people find something important or even sacred when they feel this sense of deep profoundness. Because of this, important things tend to be hidden. Throughout Japanese history, we have been attempting various ways to create this sense of depth in almost everything from language to architecture: the more the person is important, the more indirect the language becomes. Or in Shinto (our native religion), shrines are hidden in woods – even in busy cities – unlike churches, which act as a central point in many European towns. As a result of this cultural depth, expressions can appear as vague, indirect, connotative, obscure and ambiguous. As the methods they take create this sacred or profound atmosphere, the methods themselves become important rather than what is actually hidden beyond.

It is often said that what is behind these thoughts is in fact the Japanese sense of 'nature'. I myself have never been taught directly about 'nothingness' or even any other notions of culture in Japan, but I feel that naturally I have obtained these sensibilities and views by living in Japan, living as a part of its nature.

Living in a different culture now, it seems to me that making things is the way I can connect myself back to my inherited culture.

Yoko Izawa

NOTES

1. Soetsu Yanagi, Bi no Homon, Shunjyusha, Tokyo, 1980.

2. Leonard Koren, *Wabi-Sabi for Artists, Designers, and Poets and Philosophers*, Stone Bridge Press, California, 1994.

3. Leonard Koren, *Wabi-Sabi for Artists, Designers, and Poets and Philosophers*, Stone Bridge Press, California, 1994.

4. Fumihiko Maki, Kioku no Keisyou, Chikuma Shobou, Tokyo, 1992.

RIAN DE JONG

STUDIO PHILOSOPHY
You can go East or West but at Home
you will still feel best.

Rian de Jong is that most unusual of jewellers – the travelling artist, sailing round the world while still making, still creating. Having swapped her permanent bench in a well-appointed studio in one of the most desirable new parts of Amsterdam to go on an extended voyage, she has nevertheless continued to create jewellery on board and on the move. That in itself must have greatly influenced how she went about her work, given the constraints of space and movement. Yet, her fascination with materials is still very evident. These have been sourced in new locations, perhaps in shops and stores she might previously never have expected to encounter. For her they have to be different and not readily available, so travelling the world is a great way of sourcing interesting and intriguing new stuff.

Travelling is not new to her; she has previously undertaken international residencies which have taken her away from home to live in other countries for periods of time, but this high-seas voyaging is an altogether more serious undertaking, requiring detailed advance planning and extensive seafaring experience and expertise. She thinks of the constraints of a tiny constantly moving studio not so much a handicap as an open window to the biggest studio she could imagine, as this new maritime world exposes itself to her every day. As she orientates, reorientates, adapts, and feels transformed by the experience so the title of her work, 'North, East, South, West – 4 Directions' is not only a literal description of the journey but a metaphor, perhaps for the adaptability and versatility of her creative self.

BELOW
"Home Sweet Home" teapot.

OPPOSITE
"Hunted 5" brooch. Copper, glass.
50 x 50 x 10 mm.

She describes the tactile qualities of the fur which she used and how that excited creative thoughts and actions. Her reaction to seeing a cardboard tree intended for one project sitting next to a piece of fur for another is a fine example of how an action can often just happen intuitively without any premeditation: thinking-in-action which often results in unexpected outcomes. Being open to such chance occurrences and profiting from them is part of the talent of the artist.

RIAN DE JONG

THE MAKING OF 'NORTH, EAST, SOUTH, WEST – 4 DIRECTIONS'

Working in your own studio is different from working elsewhere. In your studio you have everything you need, or you know where to get it, and you feel nice, comfortable and safe. In any other situation you need to improvise, get used to the place, create a workspace.

I think I should first introduce my life in order to best describe the 'making of'.

Since I have been working as a full-time jeweller (graduated 1985) I have been travelling and working abroad and I have found myself in a variety of situations. I was invited to work for the Olympics 1994 in Norway, as an Artist in Residence in Vienna, Sidney, Idar-Oberstein and New York; all new situations with a new environment, ideas and materials to work with.

When I left Holland in 2007 to cross the ocean to Greenland and Labrador, ending up in New York for the winter months, I did not realise that for the time being I would be working in the smallest studio you can imagine. Since I have always travelled extensively, it was not too much of a challenge to create a place to work.

Normally I would always come back to the familiar surroundings of my studio in Amsterdam. Now this has changed, my partner Herman and I will be continuing our journey for the next couple of years, living on board our sailing boat and sailing around the Americas.

Maybe there is another way to view my small studio. While sailing at a leisurely pace, the world passes by and the adventure converts it into the biggest studio you could imagine, one which I can use as a daily source of inspiration. Every day is different; every day there is another experience.

I think I need or, at the very least, am used to changing surroundings from time to time. When I lived in Vienna for a few months, I had to explore and get acquainted with a city I didn't know.

I am certain that everyone feels this way when they study the map of a city and then set out, often ending up somewhere other than first intended because the city is much more complex than first anticipated. I found this quite fascinating and tried to think of a way to depict this in a piece of jewellery, though I had yet to come up with an idea of how to do this.

Finding the right materials is part of the quest. Objects found in interesting little shops and markets, second-hand goods – everything can be used as long as it is not something you can buy just anywhere.

In a new situation, unusual things catch your eye. Once I found a miniature teapot from a toy tea set decorated with the text 'Home sweet home'. It evoked a strong feeling of homesickness and has since become my mascot. It expresses the domesticity and familiar surroundings that I miss sometimes.

In Dutch you have a similar expression: 'Oost West, thuis best'. You can roughly translate that in English as: 'You can go East or West but at Home you will still feel best'.

Going to unusual places to find materials has the advantage that process, concept, materials and associations influence each other. It gives you more room to start working on concepts; it opens up your subconscious and allows your brain to lead your hands, uniting everyday awareness and visual research.

Another thing that struck me, when walking through Vienna, was the important role played by outdoor life; for example the heroics of a past hunt, and the evidence of these hunts that are visible throughout the city. Trophies in the form of skulls, antlers and stuffed animals impressed me and inspired me.

LEFT
"Hunted 2" brooch. Silver.
40 x 45 x 10 mm.

CLOCKWISE FROM TOP LEFT
4 Directions:
North. Fur, copper. 75 x 65 x 10 mm.
South. Fur, copper. 75 x 65 x 10 mm.
East. Fur, copper. 75 x 65 x 10 mm.
West. Fur, copper. 75 x 65 x 10 mm.

  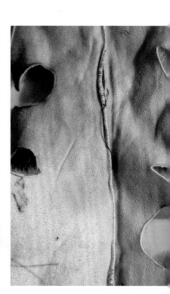

ABOVE, LEFT TO RIGHT
First try-outs on forms, not knowing what to look for really.
Looking at and playing with materials.
Cutting fur in diverse directions.
Rubber mould matrix. I don't like to use sheet material, it's too smooth. I looked for another way to create a background, and found it by using electroforming.
Heating wax for mould, in the search for how to make a background.

Altogether a concept started to grow and layers of content started to accumulate.

At the famous second-hand market, the 'Naschmarkt', I found pieces of fur from an old coat to play with. Travelling to the countryside, and walking through the woods, introduced me to an archetype of trees, similar to the shape of clubs found on playing cards. I did not recognise these trees at first, but saw them as a symbol of nature.

At this point, the tree cut out of cardboard was lying on the work table next to the fur.

Until now there had been no thought or reason to combine these two.

And then, from one moment to the next, I was cutting the same tree shape out of the fur and that was when the inspiration came to me. I could express the direction of the wind by having the hair of the fur stick out to one side. Not that this title had already crystallised in my mind, yet slowly, riding my bicycle through the city to find my way, it all came together at this one particular moment when I was cutting the fur. Just this one moment, this one action, this accidental placing together of the form and a material, made it clear.

It felt as if my hands could act beyond the control of consciousness.

What had happened?

Is it the fact that form and material were lying side-by-side, and my brain joined my hands to make the combination? Was it intuition? I don't know!

The fur I found had the bristly and shaggy character of wild boar and is particularly interesting because of the distinct way in which the hair grows in a particular direction. Cutting the fur in different ways allows you to point it in the directions of the compass: north and south, east and west. It gives you a direction to go in.

By using fur, I also refer to the harsh February cold in Vienna, and – at the same time – to the conspicuous wealth that exists in the city. People wear fur coats, which is strange for someone from Amsterdam, where fur is 'not done', yet here in the severe cold it is understandable.

If you turn the brooches around you'll see a green patinated tree. Copper not just cut from a sheet, but made by electroforming, whereby ions are built up continuously on a matrix, which might be viewed as an example of stylistic growth along with my 'travel about' way of life.

'4 Directions' brings me back to sailing too; the forces of nature, the fear of the severe winds that blow through your hair – it is all captured in this piece.

Aside from my place in Amsterdam, our ship is clearly also my home. Not the ship in itself but our way of travelling – which we have been doing over the last 30 years across a big part of our world. Staying in unknown cities – we love big cities – as long as we want, meeting people and going further in a direction we have already planned but which is not etched in stone.

To me, directions are intentions and not a goal. Nevertheless, they are necessary in my life.

For this reason, this piece is not to be considered four different brooches but in fact one.

The four brooches seen separately will give me the feeling that I am free to choose, which is only a feeling and not the truth.

Mainly Nature decides for us.

Rian de Jong

LISA JUEN

STUDIO PHILOSOPHY
My jewellery philosophy is simple: I
make jewellery because I have to.

BELOW, LEFT TO RIGHT
My sketchbook. Without it, I am
brainless.
First sketches and CAD drawing
of 'I Make You Look Sexy'.

OPPOSITE
'I Make You Look Smart'.

Lisa Juen is one of the new generation, a German who has studied in her home country and in Britain, and who chose the great adventure of starting her professional career by working for some years as a foreigner in China. It is clear from her own words that this experience of being a foreigner in a new country has greatly influenced her creative work. Her thoughts have developed around globalisation and daily life as an ex-pat observing and being partly assimilated by an alien culture. She questions, analyses, experiments with metaphor and meaning, she plays upon words. She has strong comments to make on advertising and some of the global *mores* of the day, and these brooches which she has selected to share with us are visually strong statements of her point of view.

Lisa has been intrigued by and has developed her own contemporary and very personal interpretation of 'the other'. Her approach to creating work has been methodical in parts, using drawing to record thoughts and develop ideas. For her the sketchbook is a major, indispensable tool, without which she 'is brainless', in her own words. Everything has its genesis in the drawings and notes contained in it, yet the act of making, of transforming materials, is an essential activity for her by which she also transforms inherent meanings.

Lisa is alert to the value of CAD as a development tool, which has helped express some ongoing ideas more quickly and resolved some visual problems more easily. Realising these ideas has been very much assisted by a good grounding in technical skills, which has enabled her to approach the making of her ideas with confidence. She has learnt to work with an industrial company to laser-cut the components, which she has cleverly designed to be made all in one piece. This has meant learning design skills that not all jewellery artists may need, or feel that they need, but which have nevertheless been very important in the successful realisation of her ideas into final objects. The way she has incorporated electronic components in the work is rather novel but, importantly, this is another new skill that will continue to influence her work for some time as she continues in her 'constant searching' for new answers.

LISA JUEN

STUDIO METHODOLOGY AND PHILOSOPHY

My jewellery philosophy is simple: I make jewellery because I have to.

Making things with my hands, creating ideas in my mind, expressing thoughts and resolving problems are essential to me. Making jewellery is my way of connecting with the outside world, of digesting what I see and translating the experienced information into my sort of understanding.

There are two crucial areas in my creation process: 'Conscious thinking' and 'Making'.

CONSCIOUS THINKING

For me, everything needs to make sense, needs to have a background. I need to be able to explain. I like to hide messages and play with meanings. Playing with materials and creating while seeing does not work for me.

ABOVE 'I Make You Look Sexy'.

OPPOSITE 'I Make You Look Pretty'.

BELOW
First sketches of 'I Make You Look Pretty'
and sketches and CAD drawing of 'I Make
You Look Skinny'.

to preserve their cultural image and identity, it often seems as if the West has taken over the East in terms of brands, advertising and way of life.

Being a foreigner in a country that is built on a very different culture from one's own makes it obvious what globalisation and progress can do to a country. On the one hand it is great, especially for expats, to see familiar items and goods that make it easier to adapt to the new environment, but on the other hand cultures seem to lose their edges. Character and diversity are melted into one mainstream ideal.

People in both West and East follow beauty and lifestyle ideals that are dictated by companies that want to increase sales by promising life-changing effects from buying their products. Those empty promises are reflected in the titles of my pieces, such as 'I Make You Look Pretty', 'I Make You Look Sexy', I Make You Look Skinny'. The screens show the desired goods and objects, while the carnivorous insects and plants remind us of the danger of this development.

After having drawn the first sketches of the future objects in my sketchbook, a detailed drawing needs to be generated on the computer that can be sent to the laser-cutting company. Those sketches are drawn on the computer program Illustrator.

All the pieces are made of stainless steel. The 'cold' material and 'clean' laser-cutting technique help to achieve an artificial, perfect feel in my pieces that can also be experienced in advertising. They contrast with the organic shapes of plants and insects to visualise the ambiguity of the topic.

When the cut pieces come from the laser-cutting company, they need to be cleaned, sanded and polished before all the parts can be bent into place, the stones fitted and the electronic components installed.

Lisa Juen

KADRI MÄLK

STUDIO PHILOSOPHY
An idea needs a certain level of ripeness to take its shape inside us.

BELOW
Preparatory sketches and detail of "Guilty" brooch.

OPPOSITE
"Very Guilty" brooch. Jet from Siberia – cut, carved, polished, scratched and waxed; white 14ct gold – cast, scratched, black rhodium-bathed; black spinel and two purple tourmalines from Ratna Pura – prong set. 11.5 x 6.6 x 1.2 cm.

Kadri Mälk writes poetically and mysteriously about her practice. She has an implicit understanding of what she is doing, while at the same time noting that no one is ever sure at the time of creation quite what is happening, or at least how it is happening. She is aware of her reactions and reflexes to phenomena and materials without necessarily knowing exactly why. Therein lie the mysteries and unknowns of creativity. She realises that ideas are born when they are strong and powerful enough to burst forth from the unconscious. She is aware of the necessity for patience and to fight a natural propensity to reach a quick and easy conclusion, to give in to the natural tensions inherent in the process. She realises the moment when she sees light in the forest of creative complexity which will lead to a satisfactory synthesis, and recognises the confusion and resistance to acceptance of this, with what she describes as 'redemption' and even 'resignation'.

There is clearly a serious engagement with materials and technical process. She describes making with love and passion, referring to one particular process of rubbing down jet to create dust as a valued by-product as being ritualistic in nature. Jet as a material is very dear to her; it perhaps defines her Estonian nationality as well as her personality.

She draws a lot as part of the process, exploring many variations, juxtaposing drawings against each other, sizing up the combinations of materials. She has a very sound technique, able to realise her ideas with confidence and verve, the mysteries and subconscious struggles of creation notwithstanding. Not entirely unlike Helen Britton, she uses conventional jewellery techniques in novel ways, making us question what jewellery actually is, or is not; she may make us wonder about all that powder and dust, about alternative materials. But the power of transformation is strong and effective: her jewellery could never be mistaken for anyone else's.

KADRI MÄLK

Where do art and creativity come from? Are they anticipatory? Do they stem from impulse? Or do they involve conjuring up and resuscitating something *ex post*; reconciliation, atonement?

If they are anticipatory, are they also predictive?

And if they are retroactive, would it not be inappropriate to add or ask anything more?

Asking can have a very direct impact, almost like a desire to start reconstituting one's train of thought, verify the status of one's hand and one's heart.

But it can also be a dialogue between doubt and certainty.

Diagnostic phase

No one knows why a certain idea comes to us at a certain hour and not a minute earlier. Likely an idea needs a certain level of ripeness to take its shape inside me, a certain strength to break out of the enclosing walls I have erected for myself.

But from a certain point on, there is no path of return. This is the point that must be reached.

All clear so far?

paranatellonta

Everything is already there, even in the very first mark you commit to paper, although you don't know it yet, or you know that somewhere there are hopes, concerns, passions, which oppose your first foray ... and they are spying on it, threatening to blow your cover ...

But things can go differently than planned. I can't say that it was not all preordained. It's just that I didn't know it ... it is like a letter that has been en route for a long time – written a long time ago, yet I don't recognise its contents before it reaches its addressee.

Because the process is carried out before the materialisation of jewellery takes place.

The state of being tuned in – it comes to us if we are worthy, if we have quietly sat through all that preceded it ... The intolerable state of mind.

Impatience, the mortal sin, is a tiger stalking in the thicket.

paranatellonta

Pre-attunement, a certain mood-state that creates itself, words and commands are no good, a prayer maybe ...

And yet first I swallow hard, out of a feeling of awkwardness or desperation, fear of looking in the wrong place.

paranatellonta

There are people who are not fazed by what is happening around them. It is a trait worthy of envy.

The world does its all to swallow our attention ... with the graceful melancholy of a fire-swallower.

Jet

It cannot be read in the same way as a 'real' glossy stone, an innocent one.

Microscopic examination of jet occasionally reveals the structure of petrified, fossilised coniferous wood – experienced araucarians.

OPPOSITE, CLOCKWISE FROM TOP LEFT
Detail of "Very Guilty" brooch.
"Very Guilty" and "Guilty" brooches.
Block of jet.
"Very Guilty" side detail.
"Very Guilty" reverse.
"Very Guilty" side detail.

"Guilty" brooch. Jet from Siberia – cut, carved, polished, scratched and waxed; white 14ct gold – vacuum cast, scratched, black rhodium-bathed; five spinels from Ratna Pura – bezel set.
10.1 x 6.6 x 1.1 cm.

"Very Guilty" brooch. Jet from Siberia – cut, carved, polished, scratched and waxed; white 14ct gold – cast, scratched, black rhodium-bathed; black spinel and two purple tourmalines from Ratna Pura – prong set.
11.5 x 6.6 x 1.2 cm.

The process of petrification and crystallisation is the same in both stone and a person; it is like a fare-thee-well in the human soul, a key detachment from the inessential pure alchemy.

I have worked a good bit with archaic materials, and have an unconcealed passion and affection toward them. I often give a distressed appearance to noble materials as well. Abrasion, debridement – I dealt with these techniques several decades ago. Polishing, rubbing, producing dust, my precious dust, all around me.

Wearing something down is an act of ritual power, not just a physical activity, it scores the soul, is conspicuous by its absence …

Soft velvety surface, and cosmic dust …

The dust gets thicker and slowly, very slowly, a star is born –

Gravity and the strong nuclear force are reaching compromise.

Why does the umpire whistle?

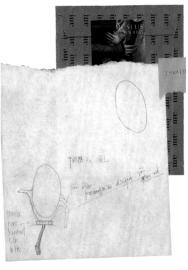

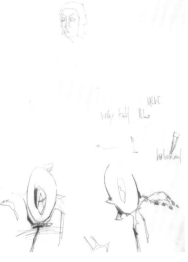

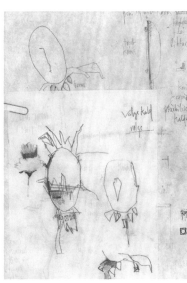

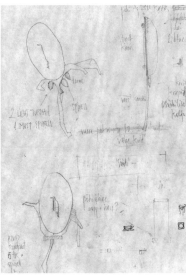

CONFUSION PHASE

Fog and dust are unquestionably the most mysterious things

on the earth for the gazer.

Honing unfocused attention, gazing ...

Constellation of dust.

Extra-terrestrial constellation?

... an unbearably beautiful silence is heard

paranatellonta

paranatellonta

There is something that binds us more than the

irreconcilable difference that separates us. Obstacle and

unreason will arise, alienation and abashment – this file does

not catch!

We are tied together as we understand the nature of choice

in the same way.

Constructive interference patterns can arise in all sorts of

places,

in imperfect condition, all sorts of life will go, but I can make

jewellery only out of me, I have nothing else.

I am interested by the technology of the soul.

How hard it is, olala, to get hold of your first person singular

...

Why does the umpire not blow his whistle?

ORIENTATION PHASE

Fertile hours loafing in the tiger's empty cage.

The readiness to awake right away and unending delay

before return to consciousness, direct experience,

orientation in your own retina,

to register the transits, the in-betweens where the borderline

is being fixed only for a fraction of tamed time.

How to tame a tiger in a thicket?

Psychosomatic process of attraction and repulsion ...

escaping of trauma, a short-circuit in the brain.

Lupus in fabula ...

Perhaps too lustful a glance at a phenomenon that is too

bright for mortals?

paranatellonta

condensed thicket of life experience, meandering run of

unfinished lines, thicket,

stimulating forest, enigmatic forest

And only the lighter patch in the treetops allows you to

discern how to get out of the forest.

paranatellonta

You have neither compass nor clocks,

time's passage can be reckoned only by the oil in the lamp

...

Why does the umpire whistle?

JUSTIFICATION PHASE

It's actually a choice between suppressed fear and

purification, fear and love.

Love me or leave me or – let me be lonely.

The wonderful violence of life which never apologises.

Resistance and redemption in silent and doleful resignation,

in full doldrums ...

saving the last traces of humility ...

A true decision makes one submissive: the one making the

decision knows that it is at the whim of many indeterminate

factors.

Chance, that pseudonym God uses when he doesn't want

to sign his own name.

Why doesn't the umpire blow his whistle now?

I feel how the chariot of Helios is steered by inexperienced

hands ...

I don't want that to happen.

Faith.

A contract with perfection, even the contract that has not

been consciously entered into, it is still binding.

Still valid.

But why does the umpire not blow his whistle?

GUILTY

Kadri Mälk

JUDY McCAIG

STUDIO PHILOSOPHY
I have an innate compulsion to move on, the continuous journey never ends.

OPPOSITE, FROM TOP LEFT
Construction of "Through a Sea of Birds":
Drawing is scratched into perspex, then carved from behind using a pendant drill.
Working out composition levels and colours.
Adding and taking away: rejecting elements and backgrounds.
Constructing the metal parts: cutting, soldering and aligning rivets with holes.
Addition of gold leaf; fitting the different sections together.
Sawing excess perspex before filing outer edge.
Final decisions on placement of elements.
Bench with works in progress.
Wires for setting made, glued in place and crystal set. Carved perspex bird riveted and painted before joining all the pieces together.

Judy McCaig is another artist who lives and works as a foreigner, a native of Edinburgh, yet domiciled in Barcelona: two very different yet internationally significant cities sited by the sea. She refers to this only obliquely, but I sense that the similarities and differences in these two cities have a (largely unspoken) significance in her work. There is a delicacy and sensitivity, a whimsicality and a freshness which at first glance might seem almost 'naive' in this work which intrigues, which pulls the viewer in to learn more, and to come to realise its depth. The drawings, which are both starting point and development tool, are just as delicate and almost fragile in their visual qualities. She talks about spontaneity in the process, very much informed by a great deal of previous experience and built-up knowledge. She talks about thinking things through in advance, of filtering ideas and making decisions which sometimes work out in reality but which sometimes do not. Like other artists featured here, drawing is only part of it: working directly with the component parts, moving them around, touching and feeling them, instinctively placing them where they belong all being equally important. That seems to be what gives most satisfaction, understanding the materials, the processes, adopting know-how from some of her other artistic practices such as printmaking, having the knowledge and confidence to grasp opportunities when some unintentional mistake unexpectedly offers what she calls 'accidental rightness'. Judy is another artist who consciously works on several pieces at a time, finding that this way of working provides the exhilaration of multiple ideas and solutions.

She refers not only to what is there but what is not, what is 'missed out'. Perhaps she is talking about deliberate decisions made during the thinking and making process; perhaps this is a reference to something realised later but which was not a conscious decision. There is a mystery about this work, which is as much about the actual physical pieces of jewellery as it is about the subject matter, the things, occurrences, and experiences which have sparked off the creative impulse.

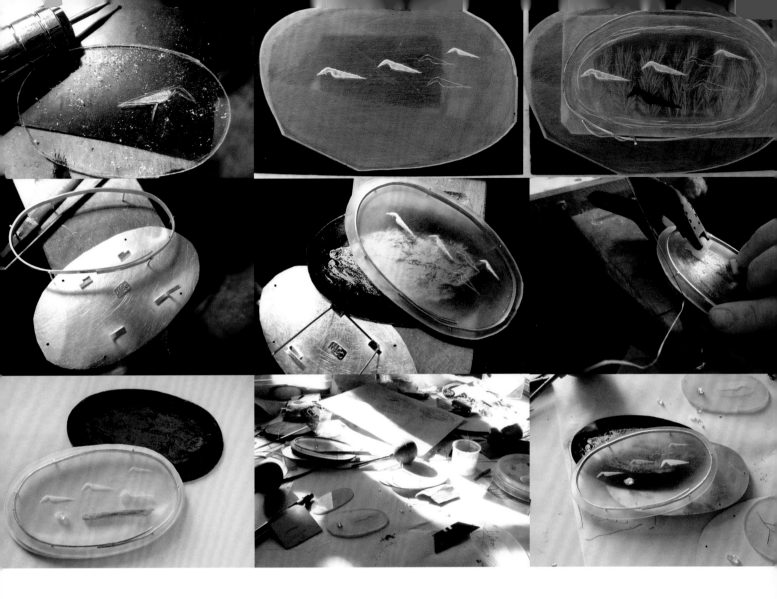

JUDY McCAIG

PHILOSOPHY

Sometimes a word, a sentence, or a poem or a story, is so resonant, so right, it causes us to remember, at least for an instant, what substance we are really made from, and where is our true home.

Clarissa Pinkola Estés

WHAT RESONATES FOR ME

Animals

*with their animal nature being gentler
than human's animal nature.
roaming creatures looking for a place
to settle.
migratory, nomadic, searching
they are the subconscious that is both
the source of art and what it speaks
to.
they are the first works of art. their
images on cave walls.
their meaning clear to the artist, but
unknown to us.
they are our first mythology.
our starting point.
struggle and intuition. survival and
instinct,
strength, weakness, vulnerability
solitary, or if in a herd, protected,
never alone*

Birds

*still standing, ready to take off, without
yet knowing where they will land,
where their
journey will take them.
restless and free.
moved by the seasons, moving with
the seasons and returning to where
they were born to
begin life's cycle again.*

Plants

*seeing the whole through the parts.
the one leaf that evokes the littered
forest floor.*

*the forest seen in a single tree.
branches moving in the wind,
flowers following the path of the sun
reaching upwards and out*

Clouds and Sea

*the same substance in different
bodies
fast-moving, ephemeral
ever-changing
never staying still,
sun breaking thru' mist,
white horses on the waves,
the haar, sea fog rolling inland,
enveloping everything in its path*

Geographical Formations

*islands with no trees,
primitive existence,
no-man's land,
rivers cutting deep gorges through
rock,
seas, mountains, lochs,
rugged coasts, barren landscapes,
still waters run deep*

Life

*travel
colours
customs
smells
people
warm rain on my face in the jungle
the view from the mountain
undiscovered villages
houses on stilts
swimming under the waterfall*

*paths through the pines
sunrise over the Mediterranean
galloping horsemen in faraway eastern
islands
night sky fading into morning
volcanic rocks rising from the sea
midnight light in the north
sheep and horses and long-haired
highland cows*

City Life

*city by the sea
buildings people pigeons
ancient shadows
history steeped
a maze of streets
cobbles
auld reekie
the chino*

Artists

*other disciplines
sometimes just a brush stroke
mark making,
inscribing, adding colour, texture,
more brush strokes,
hidden meanings, subtlety,
scoring, over painting, layers,
underneath, building up meaning and
depths
strong marks on metal
symbols, signs
blending controlled technique and
spontaneity
ancient techniques with new concepts
traditional materials with new materials*

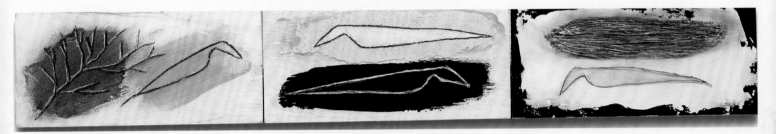

FROM TOP TO BOTTOM
"Desert Storm."
Silver, resin, perspex,
selenite, citrine, tombac,
paint, gold leaf.
"Out of the Mist, Fog and
Rain."
Mixed media, image size
36.5 x 5.5 cm; frame size
58 x 21 x 3.5 cm.
"The Light of the Moon."
Silver, perspex, paint,
crystal, selenite.
"Beyond Night Skies."
Silver, perspex.

METHODOLOGY

'Creation is like action that takes part in the present. It is building the future in the present but using the memory of the past.'

'Maybe it's okay to draw sometimes, other times there is no need because the imagination is drawing it for you. To look, to think, to consider.'

As my work has, so has my working process changed through the years. Previous work reflected the past, ancient cultures, history and future unknown. I used to transform my sketches drawn from life, from travelling, during museum visits, from nature, into exact drawings for a piece and try to reproduce it in silver and different coloured golds. Now a lot of the work goes on in my head beforehand. I solve technical solutions, work out ideas, and consider the elements I want to use. I like to let ideas filter through and hope that I manage to convey an essence of my experiences and feelings. The work evokes a different atmosphere ... lighter, timeless, ephemeral. I sketch quickly, drawing on loose paper – I can be freer than when drawing in a sketch book. I sketch many similar ideas, changing composition, size and position of the pieces. The drawings have served to outline my idea and create a direction for the work. Sometimes I have a clear idea of the elements and materials that I want to use and the piece is worked on and solved quickly, but more infrequently a piece is 'right' straightaway. Normally pieces go through countless changes before being finished. I work on several pieces at a time, I make many fragments, I turn my sketches into three dimensions and experiment with the materials and techniques that currently inspire me. I may draw into perspex, carve it, engrave formica, add paint, use enamel, resin and gold leaf, set stones or glass fragments to achieve what I need. Improvising, playing with the fragments,

THIS PAGE
"Through Night and Day."
Mixed media.

OPPOSITE
"Waiting." Mixed media.
Image size 48.5 x 5.5 cm.

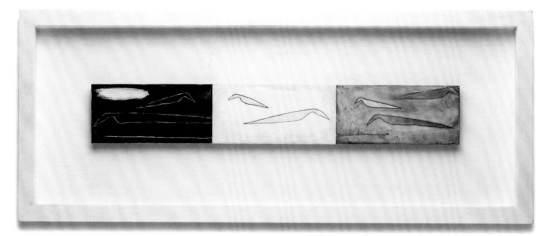

shifting shapes around, introducing new components. The results are a mixture of spontaneity, instinct and that seed of an idea. I enjoy that a piece can take or guide you places where you hadn't previously thought of going. It's great when that accidental rightness happens or a mistake makes you see another way, gives you a new idea which would never have occurred had it not been for the mistake, that fortunate accident. What is left out is essential. Making marks that are my own. I am not a neat worker, my bench and table always look like there has been an explosion.

My different working methods also apply to painting, printmaking and sculpture, which all interconnect and develop one from another; size and materials link. Painting, adding textures, mixed media, brushstrokes, rubbing out, painting over, sanding back are all techniques that I use not only in painting. Hints of images emerge, half hidden, fading, disappearing, reappearing. Drawing through resists on metal plates, etching and printing. The connections between each of the disciplines every time getting closer.

On finishing a piece, before beginning another, although I have many fragments and materials, there is still this need to go off again, knowing that I am searching for something but not sure exactly for what. I have an innate feeling/compulsion to move on, the continuous journey never ends. I enjoy this certain freedom to do what one wants to do with whatever material one wants to use. There is an element of excitement in this chaotic working process, to discover, rediscover and to create.

Judy McCaig

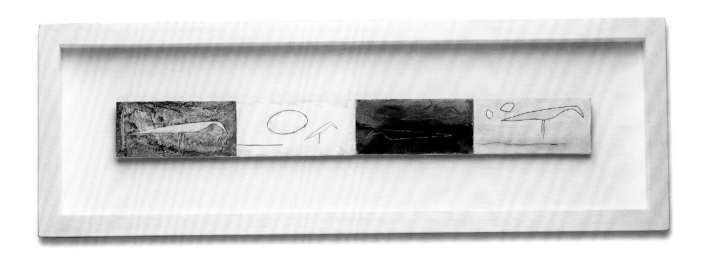

RUUDT PETERS

STUDIO PHILOSOPHY
I want to show that jewellery can also fulfil one of the most important tasks of art: to make visible what is otherwise unseen.

OPPOSITE
"Blindfold 1" sketch.

BELOW
"Anima Devota."
Anodised aluminium.
82 x 90 x 70 mm.

Ruudt Peters talks about alchemy, about transmutation of prosaic materials into a visual poetry. Greatly influenced by European and Eastern philosophy, by the male and the female in all of us, his recent projects have each addressed different aspects of these. Although each collection has been visually different and perfectly capable of being read entirely in isolation, knowing more about his preoccupations greatly informs our viewing and understanding about his philosophical approach, He makes interesting comments about how as artists we long for freedom to be ourselves, then, when we have that freedom, we can find it so hard to be truly free in what we do: we close up. To some extent this project is about opening up. To the casual observer, making forms by throwing molten wax into water and then casting or electroforming these is a very simple process; it is what first-year students used to do, after all. But that might be partly the point of this. Ruudt has reached that stage of experience, is the possessor of a vast library of tacit as well as explicit knowledge, when he can come to a technique like this with utter confidence and self-knowledge, so that whatever he does, the results he selects are perhaps simple in form but never simplistic. You might want to argue, as many artists have done before in their mature years, that 'less is more'. I think it is more complex than that in Ruudt's case: the delightful automatic drawings illustrated have both a direct and indirect relationship to the objects. They were made with exactly the same spirit of personal enquiry, yet were not intended as models for the wax: indeed, given the wax technique, it is quite impossible to control the forms in advance. There is something serendipitous happening here, yet an element of (perhaps) subconscious control as well. That, for me, is part of the mystery of Ruudt Peters' work, the Alchemy that so interests him, perhaps the intuition which Jung says is part of the Anima in us all.

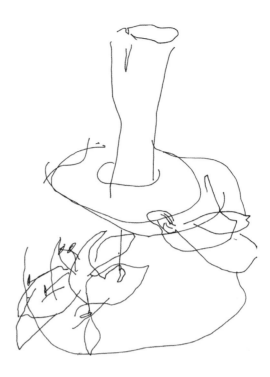

RUUDT PETERS

Alchemy has always been an inspiration for my jewellery series. My atelier is a laboratory in which all sorts of different prosaic materials can be transmuted into poetry. My recent work in the Sefiroth, Lingam and Anima series are the result of a quest for a symbolic visual language for expressing my own life experiences. I am constantly investigating the balance between West and East, between the conscious and the unconscious, between my left brain and right brain, between structure and chaos. My pieces of jewellery are rather communicative objects, and their beauty lies as much in their inner qualities as in their outward effects.

   Re-enchantment is a trend in contemporary art. It is a process of giving the world a new spiritual and holistic significance in which, among other things, there is more room for emotion, appetites, dreams and mysticism. My work would seem to fit into this. I want to show that jewellery can also fulfil one of the most important tasks of art: to make visible what is otherwise unseen.

ANIMA (2008/2010)

According to Carl Gustav Jung, Anima is the feminine in a human being: a person is both male and female. As a result of upbringing, one is developed, and the other not. Consequently a man generally develops his male side more than his female side. If the Anima in a man is underdeveloped, this hinders his functioning. Qualities ascribed to the Anima include: the Magna Mater ('Great Mother'), the source of life, Eros, goddess of love, seductive, beautiful, irrational, dreamy, begetter of illusions, constrained, natural, receptive, servant, prophetess, bringer of wisdom, and incorporeal.

After the Sefiroth series, which was strongly rooted in my personal experiences translated into the visual language of the Tree of Life, and the Lingam series that dealt with the male side of the brain, I have gone in search of the female subconscious (the ANIMA) as a guide for my designing. Since 2008 I have engaged in drawing blind, in order to obtain more freedom in my thinking. These drawings give form to an unfamiliar terrain in my visual language. I cannot direct it. My dream was to be able to make work that refers to the subconscious in the same way as the blind drawing. This would produce a totally different sort of design, in terms of freedom, thinking and expression.

Development of Anima

If you grasp at things desirously, the beauty retreats.

Augustine of Hippo

During this period in my work I have made it my goal to produce work that is not directed by reason. I let the work happen out of the subconscious, in the same way as the blind drawings. At first this was an impossible task. You want freedom, but because you are trying too hard for freedom, you clench up. Initially I tried to transpose the freedom of the line technique in the blind drawing into the object. At a certain point I gave up on this because it was a disastrous course. Then by chance I poured wax into water. The wax solidified immediately in the water. The freedom of the visual language that this creates is impossible to control. It demands great meditative concentration to pour the wax into the water at precisely the right moment, and with that to also make a drawing at the same moment. You get what it is. It is a record of a second, a congealed moment in time. Each working day yields a different image. The weather and my state of mind influence the outcome, but I

BELOW
Storyboard.

RIGHT
"Anima Arvilla."
Electroformed silver.

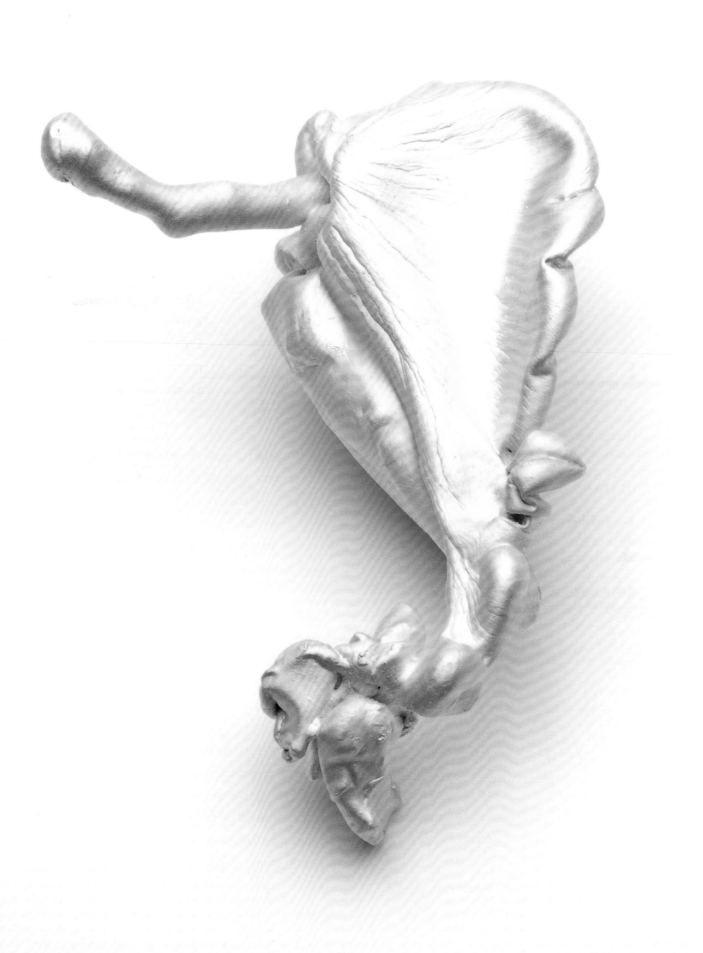

NATALYA PINCHUK

STUDIO PHILOSOPHY
The process for creating my jewellery is a bit like preparing a dinner.

OPPOSITE
"5.10" brooch. Wool, leather, copper, enamel, brass, plastic, stainless steel, 14ct gold, thread.

BELOW
Compositions.

Natalya Pinchuk has a delightful, almost poetic, way of describing how she creates. Clearly she has a love affair with her materials. One could not imagine her making anything without spending intense periods handling the materials, selecting them, moving them around like an enormously complex bench-top puzzle, trying them on, persuading others to do so and, finally, making decisions. One gets the impression of her being almost in love with the process to the extent that the journey is more important than, or at least as important as, the destination. Yet, there is more to it than that. Drawing plays its part in the process, but as a supporting activity rather than the main vehicle of creation. Indeed, a lot of the 'drawing' is done mentally as part of the early-stage thinking about the project. She is using her visual library in a different way, thinking three-dimensionally 'in the materials', as one might say. From that there seem to be so many ideas teeming about that she thinks in multiples and variations, perhaps in a more formal way than many other artists. Indeed she states that it is her very nature to be inclined to make more than one thing at a time. Out of that maelstrom of possibilities, gradually the final solutions present themselves.

She is one of those who is thinking about a potential wearer of the piece at an early stage of the project, often in quite surreal circumstances, such as when she imagines Arnold Schwarzenegger wearing an outrageously feminine brooch. Rather than being concerned simply to create a work of art which has its own *raison d'être*, wearability and practicality are important to her. That said, creation for her is a largely intuitive process, assisted by drawing but not in thrall to it. The materials are what determine the end results.

NATALYA PINCHUK

THE PROCESS

What is the process for thinking up my jewellery? Well, it's a bit like preparing a dinner. Once the menu is set, the proportion of ingredients for each dish can be varied and slight additions of this or that change the experience. And, let's not forget, preparing a dinner also implies a basic awareness of circumstance, expectations and desires. When sharing a meal with others, it is no longer about me only. Sure, I am a big part of it, but I have to make decisions that make sense not only to me but to others as well, at times gently teasing and playing with the circumstance. Who is coming for dinner? What's the occasion? What are the ambitions for this dinner? Casual, warm and friendly meal-sharing? Professional, impressive and ambitious ego-stroking? Provocative and seductive propositions? Status-affirming? Cooked to impress? I think you get the point … And of course, once the contextual undercurrents are decided on, which ingredients are needed for the chosen meal? And what is available to me?

So far, my jewellery-making enterprise has been heavily grounded within academic settings where the university, the gallery, the collector and the museum were my dinner mates. These were the individuals and institutions for whom I laboured and with whom I wished to share a meal. These were the dinner mates for whom I cooked up the new and the unexpected, obliging with meals full of colour, vibrancy and surprise. This bit of information sets the table, so to speak, and honestly

identifies an undercurrent of the jewellery I am about to introduce you to.

Before I delve into the particulars, I would like to note that in all my jewellery devising, my main ingredients are simple: material probing and thoughts. The ingredient I call 'thoughts' is just that – clear notions and goals. These notions heavily drive and constrain the formal choices. The material explorations, on the other hand, are playful and experimental in nature, without a necessarily clear objective, communicating accidentally and haphazardly at first, until interpretations and impressions emerge. The proportions of one ingredient to the other change with circumstance and mood, but both are present in any making process. The bulk of the jewellery and manner of working that I would like to share rely heavily on material exploration, with thoughts acting as supporting ingredient. This process consists of several stages happening in a rather organic manner, referencing each other and repeating when necessary.

Let me also add that my process relies on multiples and sheer variation of a given. When tasked to make one piece of jewellery, my nature calls me to start making five, all stemming from the same core. That is why I will be referring to the jewellery piece whose development I am tasked to elucidate as brooches in plural rather than singular.

EFFECT

My design process begins with two simple tasks: clarifying the most basic effects I want my jewellery to have on the viewer and wearer, as well as envisioning the format that suits these inclinations (brooch, ring, necklace …). I literally sit down and imagine the kinds of situations in which I want my jewellery to be worn. What reactions would it please me to draw from people? Often, to jump-start the process I simply ask myself: 'wouldn't it be great if …?' For example, wouldn't it be great to imagine the most conservative heterosexual men in today's world all of a sudden wearing something utterly opposite to their present uniform – brooches that are feminine, delicate, luscious and sexually charged? Then an image of a Schwarzenegger type coming out onto a stage pops into my head. He is on TV, ready to give a speech, wearing a large gorging hot pink fruity brooch or a flowering tongue. This makes me smile and I know I am onto something. By conjuring up particular scenarios, I am able to narrow down to the simplest of terms what I wish my jewellery to embody on immediate emotional and intelligible levels. While at times contradictory and lighthearted, these words and short phrases represent clearly and succinctly my wants for the jewellery. I need these simple goals and images to begin; without them I am lost.

THIS PAGE
"2.10" brooch. Wool, silver, gold,
copper, enamel, leather, waxed
thread, stainless steel.
32 x 14 x 4.5 cm.

OPPOSITE
"14.09" brooch, modelled and
close-up. Wool, copper, enamel,
leather, plastic, waxed thread and
stainless steel.
78 x 13 x 9 cm.

First thoughts that should pop into an onlooker's head: bold, soft, rough, sensual, seducing, commanding, luscious, eerie, naughty, jarring, decadent, dangerous, delicate, feminine …

What should the wearer feel or think? in control, empowered, centre of attention, playful, teasing, alive …

What should the onlookers experience? slight discomfort, attraction, surprise, an itch to touch, stare …

ABOVE
Warm-up: visual reference materials.

OPPOSITE
Parts: daydreaming with objects and materials.

Warm-up

My next step is to look at reference materials that I find curious and appropriate – images of flowers, snakes, rodent tails, tongues, insects, fruits, leaves, genitals, flamboyant desserts, seeds, etc. While looking I make quick sketches of details and forms I find particularly interesting. I then sketch quick designs as warm-up exercises and vary intriguing forms until nothing else comes to mind. Once this stage is exhausted, I put the visual references away. I stop sketching and am ready to make ….

Parts

I pull out boxes of stuff from storage and lay the contents across the tables and floor to see if any of the kept materials, objects and parts are useful. If necessary, I search for other options. In the beginning as I make forms and texture bits, I reference the original brainstorming results. Eventually, the process becomes about variation on top of variation as I try to exhaust the possibilities of a given. Throughout all of this, I imagine how the finished pieces might look, other possible materials and methods of construction, but no final decisions are made at this point, no pressures are exerted. More ideas and variations come to mind. I call this daydreaming. This is a lovely, non-committal and exploratory period.

Compositions

Eventually deadlines approach, ideas get exhausted, hands get tired but confidence grows and a desire for something complete and cohesive emerges. I clean and organise my working area while categorising the numerous parts and samples. When all seems in order, I make a series of intuitive arrangements until several begin to feel right. I snap a couple of photos and rearrange again. In due course, I pin the arrangements on my husband's chest, evaluating whether the initial characteristics are present, whether the list of brainstormed words springs to mind. Nothing feels right at first, but eventually parts fall into place and satisfying brooch compositions materialise. I am content. I pin the final arrangement on my husband's chest again and ask him to dance around the room, testing how the brooch responds to movement. I assemble the parts and take the brooch for a spin around the house myself.

That's it.

Natalya Pinchuk

PETER SKUBIC

STUDIO PHILOSOPHY
The concept of jewellery as having a function only when being worn is something I abhor.

OPPOSITE
The mercury ring, melting.

BELOW
Brooch. Stainless steel, glass, wire.

Peter Skubic has delighted, teased and challenged us for a lifetime. As comfortable using non-precious as precious metals, he is known for precisely engineered and sometimes very complex works in stainless steel as well as gold. He creates objects on a domestic scale as well as jewellery on a personal one. His recent work, which used the Fibonacci sequence in conjunction with his impressive knowledge of structural principles as the vehicle for design, was very well documented and made a considerable impact. He describes having learned to be an artist as a consequence of his original training as an engraver. As long ago as the 1970s he explored body modification through experimentation with subcutaneous stainless steel implants. However, as he notes in his statement, he wanted to be represented in this volume by something that he created a few years ago and which, by its very nature, is totally unrepeatable. The mercury ring must have been a dangerous undertaking, not something to emulate or replicate, given the health risks involved; but it is a testament to the immense technical and personal confidence he demonstrates. Although Peter normally uses drawing as part of his creative process – he sees it as a means of thinking – in this project the work was done directly with the materials.

Obviously the entire process was planned very carefully. Working with mercury is dangerous and can result in serious damage to health, so it was important that all likely dangers were considered and allowed for, that the process was planned in such a way that as far as possible those dangers were reduced to make creation safe for the artist. This project is not about the physical experience of direct working in the sense of touching the material, but rather of a lifetime of studio practice that provided the skills and expertise to know exactly what to do at the right time, and exactly how to do it. Thus, through a very particular form of technical mastery and self-confidence, he has been able to make a three-dimensional statement which challenges us to consider and reconsider the nature of jewellery and our preconceptions of it as something inimitably wearable. Whereas some artists believe that jewellery is only jewellery when it is worn, he is adamant that jewellery is jewellery – whatever.

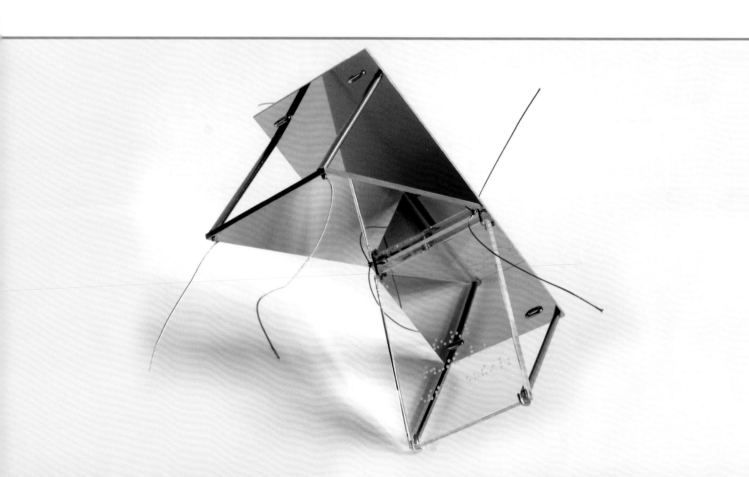

PETER SKUBIC

Mirrors are not visible – cloudy mirrors can be seen.

The concept of jewellery as having a function only when being worn is something I abhor.

A car is a car also when it is parked, and I would not judge the quality of a painting by its size matching the space above the couch. There are more pieces of art stored in depots than are displayed or in use.

I am fascinated by the invisible, the non-existing, the envisioned, the transient, and the things behind.

I like to get to the bottom of things.

Since 2000 my pieces of jewellery have been made of mirroring stainless-steel surfaces. They are mostly brooches. The mirroring surfaces reflect their surroundings, confronting the viewer with changing visual appearances. The surfaces themselves are invisible – like mirrors, which also have never been seen by a human. Not to speak of blind people: for them, everything is invisible. Visual sense makes up only a small part of our perceptive abilities. A brooch I made in 2007 consists of two high-gloss stainless-steel surfaces and one rock-crystal panel. Into the latter, the following is milled in Braille: 'Blinde können das nicht lesen' ('Blind people cannot read this'). The milling was done on the reverse side of the rock-crystal panel and it is so delicate that it is not palpable – not perceptible, even for those who see and who are not proficient in Braille. That is the message behind it: we see so little because we do not perceive – understand.

Making the mercury ring: making a mould, pouring liquid mercury into the mould, waiting for it to solidify and cooling it in carbon dioxide snow. The solid ring is then removed from the mould and left to return to room temperature, at which it begins to melt and lose its form.

On 1 April 2000, I made a ring of mercury. Mercury is a metal which, under normal conditions on our planet Earth, is in a liquid state of aggregation that is quite fascinating. Instead of melting metal, pouring it into the casting mould and waiting for it to solidify, I poured mercury into the mould, cooled it in carbon dioxide snow and removed the now-solid metal from the mould. One can look at the ring – that is what it is – until it returns to normal temperature, melts, and loses its form. The form is only a memory.

Since I started making jewellery, I have been confronted with one question: What is jewellery? Is it the content and meaning – the theme – that is significant? More significant than form? What are the limits for the dimensions of jewellery and its weight, so as to be still wearable? A work by Manfred Nisslmüller from 1987 is entitled 'Die Garnitur' ('The Set'). Earrings, ring, brooch, bracelet and choker necklace are cast in lead: 2 kg for the earrings and up to 42.2 kg for the choker necklace, which makes us seriously question their wearability.

My first piece of jewellery, a pendant, was made of stainless steel, and I have stuck with stainless steel as the material I use most. It gives me the option of making larger pieces of work, by far surpassing the dimensions of jewellery.

Since 1973, I have been working with tension. I fit together individually constructed parts and fix them with compression and tension springs or magnets. I increase the strength of the tension with levers.

A friend made me realise that tension was my inner state of mind at that time. It resulted in brooches, rings and objects of greater dimensions, culminating in a tower of 4 metres.

The fascination of the early Cycladic marble sculptures inspired me to deal with the topic of 'idols' in terms of tension. A total of ten pieces have resulted from this series – two brooches, two large sculptures and six medium-sized pieces. The proportions of a piece of work are most decisive for me. So I made more than eighty sketches at first, in order to get a better understanding of this series' proportions.

Proportions are an important factor of human feeling and understanding, be it in music, literature, painting or sculpture. Proportions decide about good or bad and determine optical tension in visual arts.

The intrinsic secret as an inherent inventory of jewellery is not to be under-estimated. It might be good-luck charms, such as photos, hair or other things enclosed in medallions. In my case, it is names of women who I like to remember, or the piece of jewellery itself represents the encoded name of its owner. In the first case, it is a series of rings, where the whole length of the ring band is engraved with the name in an anamorphic way. 'Anamorphic' means 'changing the form', in this case to lengthen the letters. One order for a custom-made chain inspired me to design the name of the owner in longer and shorter chain links, according to the Morse code. The client was a long-serving railway man. In former times, all higher ranking railway officials needed to know the Morse code.

By using the Fibonacci numbers as a basis for encoding, one can get more accidental proportions. For this purpose, I write the beginning of the number sequence up to 8, that is 1, 1, 2, 3, 5 and 8, then I write the alphabet in four rows below, assigning a different colour to each row. This way, a number and a colour is established for each character. This system is suitable for the brooches with mirroring surfaces. The colour design of the reverse sides of the differently sized surfaces is formulated according to this coding system.

The invisible also means the non-existing, such as pedestals for invisible, since non-existing, pieces of jewellery, which I have occasionally made since 1990. These pedestals are painted, thus giving a clue to the imaginary piece of jewellery on them.

Can one minimise NOTHINGNESS? Does a plausible 'LESS THAN NOTHING' exist?

If, on a card, I write the words LESS THAN NOTHING, and then I punch a hole in the card, cutting away part of the word NOTHING, thus the word NOTHING has become reduced – it has become less, that is, LESS THAN NOTHING.

A cosmic black hole is invisible, too. In 1991 I made an art print on paper which says: 'The Black Hole Is The Inside Of The Ring Of God'.

The 12-piece series 'The Inside of a Ring' from 1985, printed on photo paper, describes the closeness and different states of a ring, but never a specific ring. There is, for example, a black sheet entitled 'Ring bei Nacht ohne Licht') (Ring by Night

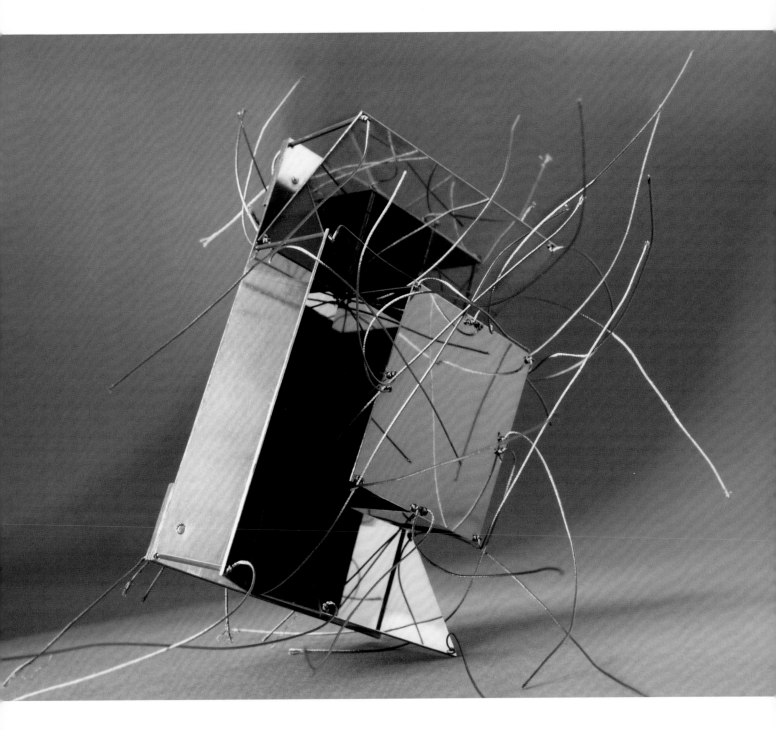

Without Light); or a very small black square on a white background: 'Ring bei Nacht ohne Licht – weit weg' (Ring by Night Without Light – Far Away). 'Das Innere eines Ringes' (The Interior of the Ring) is a small black circle on a white background. There is also 'Ein gedachter Ring auf einem nicht vorhandenen Blatt' (A Ring Thought Up on a non-existing Sheet) and so on.

Peter Skubic

GRAZIANO VISINTIN

STUDIO PHILOSOPHY
Vocation to geometry creates the
quality of shape in apparently simple
objects.

OPPOSITE
Rings. Gold, enamel, niello.

BELOW
Brooch. Gold, silver,
oxidised copper and niello.
120 x 40 x 37 mm.

Graziano Visintin is a well-established Italian jeweller who trained at the renowned Pietro Sylvatico Institute in Padova, thus following in a long line of distinguished creators and a tradition of refined jewellery which, at its best, is much more than it sometimes might seem, sometimes spectacularly virtuosic, sometimes deceptively simple in form yet full of underlying subtlety. Given the very sound technical nature of the training there, it is no surprise that Graziano has a fascination for precious metal and demonstrates a mastery of traditional goldsmithing techniques. This is married with a visual sensitivity and sense of refinement in how he approaches his work. He has a knowledge and awareness of historical precedents, both technical and aesthetic, with the result that his work is profoundly informed by his deep understanding of traditional hand skills and historical metallurgical phenomena. His studio methodology is a deceptively straightforward one in that he utilises drawing throughout, in recording and manifesting the original ideas and then, in conjunction with 'soft' models such as paper and card, gradually refines the ideas until the final realisation. He talks about being fascinated by geometric forms and interpreting the expressive potential of apparently simple elements, and about having what he describes as a 'vocation to geometry'.

The seemingly simple geometric forms which emanate from the particular project illustrated here are certainly not simplistic, but rather the ultimate in refinement in terms of his particular practice. As we shall see in the work of others, there is a stage in an artist's career when complexity and embellishment become less important. There is a confidence in the understanding of all that has gone before and no need to make things unnecessarily difficult. The simple statement is more subtle and profound perhaps than the obviously complex. Often enough, the apparently simple visual statement is the result of very sophisticated and refined thinking, of an aesthetic rigorously applied. Visintin strives to distil a simplified and yet subtle visual meaning from geometry.

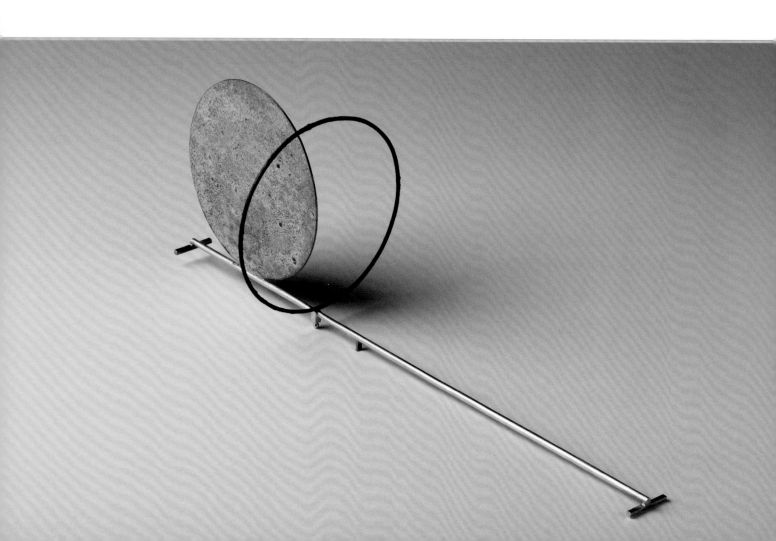

GRAZIANO
VISINTIN

LA GEOMETRIA DELL'ORO (THE GEOMETRY OF GOLD)

I studied the goldsmith's art from 1968 to 1973 at the Pietro Selvatico Institute of Art in Padova, where I studied under Mario Pinton, Francesco Pavan and Giampaolo Babetto, in whose studio I worked for two years.

I have been teaching laboratory and workshop techniques at the same institute since 1976.

At first, my works were configured as a reduction of shape and volume, where solids lose their mass yet preserve their outline. Primary geometrical elements such as squares, triangles, circles and ovals aligned, criss-crossed or superimposed, confronting the compactness of gold, an element that was never abandoned even when ebony and ivory were used.

Gold has always fascinated me. It is a precious material, not so much for its pecuniary value, but for its characteristics of workability (malleability and ductility), and therefore requires the utmost attention.

In the eighties, shapes were elongated, emptied, dematerialised to the point of becoming brilliant light.

MIZUKO YAMADA

STUDIO PHILOSOPHY
I aim to make jewellery that casts a
lovely spell on people.

OPPOSITE
Preparatory sketch.

BELOW
"Jewellery to Assist Contact" bangle.
145 x 125 x 73 mm.

Mizuko Yamada is, unusually nowadays, both jeweller and silversmith. The project which she has selected for this book is a perfect example of the symbiotic relationship between both activities. The daughter of a sculptor father and a mother (Reiko Yamada) who was one of the first wave of post-war Japanese contemporary jewellers, she was brought up to the sound of metalwork of one sort or another. As one might expect from an artist who has been educated in the Japanese traditions of fine metalwork, her output is exceedingly refined. Outwardly simple, bold, and almost modest in appearance, it repays looking at again and again. This is work that has evolved through several years of constant application and hard work as well as an underlying talent to reach this level of apparently effortless existence. This jewellery is informed very much by Mizuko's interest in social and talismanic relationships within the national cultural context. In a society which is outwardly generally reserved, very well-mannered, and undemonstrative, the question of how to open up conversations and initiate relationships is often unresolved. Thus, her activities as a silversmith making hollowware have influenced her approach to jewellery, whereby the idea of handles which can be worn and which will tempt others – strangers presumably – to hold onto them, was born. In realising this idea, drawing, tactility, surface qualities, and form all influence her practice. She draws carefully and precisely, as if the ideas have largely been 'designed' already as part of a thinking process which sees very clearly in three dimensions. Working directly with the metal, 'feeling' the sound of hammer on metal as it travels up the arm and through the body, making decisions about minor changes as she goes along, all seem to be what really engage her in the creative process as initial ideas are finally refined and elegant solutions arrived at.

MIZUKO YAMADA

Twenty years have passed since I started my career as a jeweller.

I started during my undergraduate years at art university, by making jewellery
with reliefs of my favourite faces by chasing flat metal panels. After this I studied
silversmithing as a postgraduate. I was always in pursuit of originality in my jewellery,
exploiting the silversmithing raising technique that is rarely used in making jewellery.
Ten years ago, I finally found my own theme, 'tactile form'. Since then, using metals,
I have been making jewellery of a smooth texture that communicates itself visually
without even a touch.

While I continuously pursue making jewellery with tactile forms, I made a new
experiment a few years ago: I started to consider the relationship between jewellery
and the wearer as well as the wearer and viewer.

I was busy making pieces for an exhibition, and this time I made many pots. I like
my style of making pots where the surface continues from its body to the handle.
There are many handle parts for pots on my workbench.

At first, I thought about making a handle for the back of a man, a handle like a
strap on a train. This would be jewellery for men with the purpose of luring others

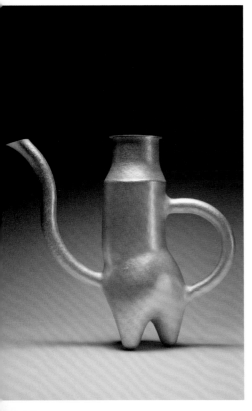

towards him. But actually, it is difficult to put a simple handle on a human body, a complex support like armour would be needed. However, from this grew the idea of connecting two people with jewellery. I liked the idea that one person wears the jewellery and the other person catches hold of it, and as a result they make a connection. I started thinking about typical actions for connecting two people such as shaking hands.

The 'Jewellery to Assist Contact' bangle is a new proposal for jewellery, not as decoration, or to display fine materials, or to charm by interesting form, but jewellery designed as a tool to connect one person with another. Usually, jewellery provides a chance for connection through conversation between people, or by making an emotional connection by using matching jewellery such as wedding rings. However, this piece symbolically shows the connection between people by using jewellery to physically connect two people as if they were joining hands.

The 'Jewellery for Contact Awareness' bangle is for use by one person, to promote awareness of contact or connection through the sense of touch, as if you were shaking hands with the jewellery. Unlike traditional jewellery, the main purpose of this work is not to decorate the figure, but to act as a tool for thinking sensitively about contact or connection by the wearer alone.

There are many dark topics in the news of our contemporary society, the September 11th disaster and its aftermath, the spread of war and economic crisis, the increasing numbers of the weak and disadvantaged in society. I think it is a very important time to reconsider the connection between others, not to compete and survive by oneself alone.

Jewellery is a field most typically recognised for luxurious ornament. It has been charming mankind, both physically and emotionally, throughout history with its material value and beauty. I feel it has at times been a tool for cutting the connection between people more than connecting people, with the exception of some items such as wedding rings or family heirlooms. One of the oldest pieces of jewellery in the world is a pendant of animal bone, made in China tens of thousands of years ago. It served as a talisman for our remote ancestors, to help them stand up to powerful animals and the harsh environment. Today, expanding on the past traditions of this ancient art form, many contemporary jewellery artists are searching for new reasons for the existence of jewellery.

Now I have come to my mid-career and sometimes contemplate complex matters for the concept when working on pieces. My all-time favourite, however, is a tiny silver ring with a glass stone, though now it is too small even for my little finger. My

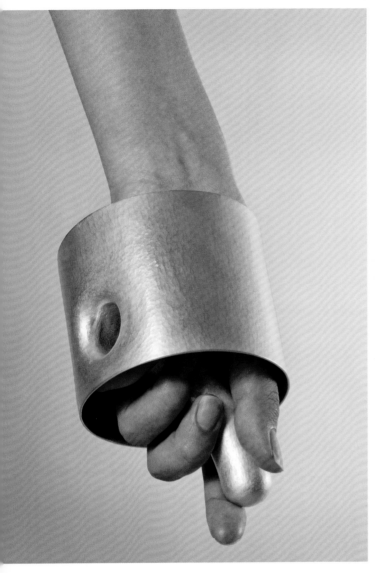

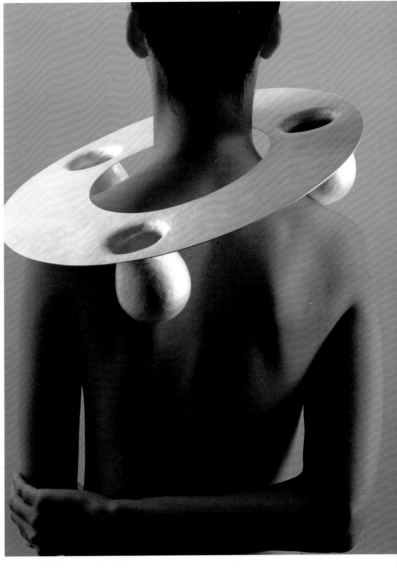

OPPOSITE TOP
Teapot. Silver-plated copper.

OPPOSITE BELOW
Detail: teapot handle.

ABOVE LEFT
"Jewellery for Contact
Awareness" bangle.
85 x 105 x 85 mm.

ABOVE RIGHT
Necklace. Silver-plated
copper.
400 x 80 x 400 mm.

father made it for me when I was about three years old. It was a magic ring. Just putting it on my finger to complete my dressing for special outings, a bad-tempered and annoying girl would quickly be replaced by a lady.

I aim to make jewellery that casts a lovely spell on people.

The bangle is made from four pieces of flat copper sheet. First, I made a simple bangle from a rectangular piece of copper, joining the two ends with TIG welding. I then made the interior handle part from a strip of copper, hammering the metal into a slightly curved pipe shape with a doming hammer on a sandbag, and then welding the seam closed. I made a copper cap for the end of the handle with a doming punch and welded them together. I hammer-raised a circular piece into a cone shape and used this to join the bangle and the handle together, welding and then planishing the form over stakes. This was the most difficult part, but crucial to make the four pieces feel as one. I hammered over the handle again to smooth out the shape and make sure the separate pieces flow together. I used a slightly textured planishing hammer that gives my work a characteristic surface quality. Finally the copper piece was cleaned and silver plated. I like the colour of silver-plated copper, whiter than sterling, another colour in the metal palette.

Mizuko Yamada

RIGHT
Bangles.
Silver-plated copper.

FAR RIGHT
"Quake" rings

AFTERWORD

So, each of the jewellers featured in this book has a very individual approach to creating their work. There are seventeen different 'jewelleries' and seventeen different 'methodologies'. I put these words in inverted commas because I think some of the artists would probably take issue with the use of the word methodology, preferring to think of what they do as being a much freer and more spontaneous activity than the word might suggest. However that may be, what I believe binds them together is their great concern for the materials they choose to use, their interest in the materiality of objects, the transformation they effect in the materials they use, the new life they give to them, by virtue of the highest levels of craftsmanship and creativity – not blindly making to a pre-ordained template, but thinking through making, applying individual philosophies, personal intellect, active intuition, sensitivity, continuously enquiring and experimenting, and immense passion for the one thing they exist to do: make jewellery.

Norman Cherry, Lincoln

'... keep practising. After a great deal of practice, we no longer think about the necessary movements we must make; they become part of our existence. Before reaching that stage, however, you must practise and repeat. And if that's not enough, you must practise and repeat some more'.

The character of Nabil Alaihi in *The Witch of Portobello* (2007), Paulo Coelho. London: Harper Collins.

ARTISTS' CVs

EDUCATION/TRAINING

2005	Diplom. Akademie of Fine Art, München, Germany
1999–2003	Akademie of Fine Art, München, in Prof. Otto Künzli's class for Jewellery and Objects
1998	Guest studies at the Sandberg Institute, Amsterdam, Netherlands
	Guest studies at San Diego State University, San Diego, USA
1997–1999	MFA, Curtin University of Technology, Perth, Australia
1997–1998	Guest studies at the Akademie of Fine Art, München, in Prof. Otto Künzli's class for Jewellery and Objects
1995	Honours (1st class) Curtin University of Technology, Perth, Australia
1990–1994	BA Edith Cowan University, Perth, Australia

AWARDS

2010	The Australia Council: Development Assistance
2009	Luitpold Stipendium, München, Germany
2007	Erfurt City Goldsmith
2006	Bavarian State Prize, International Handwerksmesse, München, Germany
	Project grant for Fine Art from the city of München, Germany
2005	Academy of Fine Art, München, Germany: DAAD-Prize for Foreign Students
	International Handwerksmesse, München, Germany: Herbert Hofmann Prize

COLLECTIONS

The Art Gallery of South Australia, Adelaide, Australia
Stichting Françoise van den Bosch, Amstelveen, Netherlands
Stedelijk Museum, Amsterdam, Netherlands
Auckland Museum, Auckland, New Zealand
Queensland Art Gallery, Brisbane, Australia
National Gallery of Australia, Canberra, Australia
Die Neue Sammlung, Staatliches Museum für angewandte Kunst, München (Dauerleihgabe der Danner-Stiftung)
The Art Gallery of Western Australia, Perth, Australia
Curtin University of Technology, Perth, Australia
Schmuckmuseum im Reuchlinhaus, Pforzheim, Germany
The Powerhouse Museum, Sydney, Australia
The National Gallery of Victoria, Australia

SOLO EXHIBITIONS

2010	Wet, Glittering Dark, Shiny, Pointy, Sharp, Galerie Louise Smit, Amsterdam, Netherlands
2009	Somewhere Else Completely, Bavarian Crafts Council, München, Germany
2008	Chaos and Clean Shapes, Klimt02 Gallery Barcelona, Spain
	The Things I See, Gallery Funaki, Melbourne, Australia
2006	Urban Paradise Playground, Objectspace, Auckland, New Zealand
2005	Second Nature, Galerie Louise Smit, Amsterdam, Netherlands
2004	Crisscrossing, Galerie Hélène Porée, Paris, France

GROUP EXHIBITIONS

2008	The Fat Booty of Madness, Pinakotech der Moderne, München, Germany
2007	Field of Vision, Sofa Gallery, Indiana University, Bloomington, USA
2006	Pattern recognition, Object Gallery, Sydney, Australia
2005	Choice: Contemporary Jewellery from Germany, Museum of Arts and Crafts, Itami; Galerie YU, Hiko Mizuno College, Tokyo, Japan; Schmuckmuseum im Reuchlinhaus, Pforzheim, Germany (travelling exhibition); Pensieri preziosi 2, Gioielli senza confini, Oratorio di San Rocco, Padova, Italy

SELECTED PUBLICATIONS

Helen Britton: Jewellery Life. O. O., 2010
The Fat Booty of Madness, Arnolsche, Germany, 2008
Field of Vision Indiana University, Bloomington, USA, 2007
Helen Britton is the City Goldsmith in: GZ Art + Design, *International Jewelry* Magazine 2007, Nr. 2 (May), 95
Lupton Ellen, *'Framing: The Art of Jewelry'*, in: Metalsmith 2007, Vol. 27, Nr. 4, curated Exhibition in Print, 14/15
Holzach Cornelie (Hrsg.), *Kunst treibt Blüten*, Schmuckmuseum im Reuchlinhaus, Pforzheim. Stuttgart, 2007
Helen Britton: Urban Paradise Playground, Objectspace, Auckland, 2006

SIGURD BRONGER

EDUCATION/TRAINING
Oslo Yrkesskole, jewellery department, Norway
MTS Vakschool Schonhooven, Netherlands

EMPLOYMENT/SELF-EMPLOYMENT
Engraver at the Koninklijke Stempel Fabrieken Posthumus, Amsterdam, Netherlands
Technical Engineer at Norwegian Broadcast Company NRK

AWARDS
2010	Norsk Form Design award 'Jacob Prize'
2001	Art and Craft Jubilee Award
1997	Norwegian Design Award
1995	Norwegian Art and Craft Award
1992, 1994, 1997, 2004	Norwegian Goldsmiths Award

COLLECTIONS
Pinakothek der Modern, Die Neue Sammlung, München, Germany
Victoria and Albert Museum, London, UK
Stedelijk Museum, Amsterdam, Netherlands
Lillehammer Art Museum, Lillehammer, Norway
Middlesbrough Institute of Modern Art, UK
Design Museum Copenhagen, Denmark
The National Museum, Stockholm, Sweden
The National Museum of Art and Design, Oslo, Norway
SM-s Stedelijk Museum 's-Hertogenbosch, Netherlands
Design Museum, Helsinki, Finland
The Art Museum of Northern Norway
National Museum of Decorative Art, Trondheim, Norway
Royal College of Art, London, UK
The Rockefeller Foundation, New York, USA

SOLO EXHIBITIONS
2011	Lillehammer Art Museum, Lillehammer, Norway
2006	Galerie RA, Amsterdam, Netherlands
2005	National Museum, Stockholm, Sweden
2001	Bergen Kunsthall, Bergen, Norway
1999	Galerie RA, Amsterdam, Netherlands
1998	Ram Galleri, Oslo, Norway

GROUP EXHIBITIONS
2010	Body Stories 'Chi ha Paura?' Stedelijk Museum 's-Hertogenbosch, Netherlands
2009	Lingam, Konstfack, Stockholm, Sweden
2007	Romancing the stone, Manchester Town Hall, UK
2001	Micromegas, Bayerischer Kunst gewerbe-Verein, München, Germany
2000	The Ego Adorned, Koningin Fabiolazaal, Belgium
1997, 1988, 2001, 2004, 2006, 2010	Schmuck
1995, 2004	Nordic Jewellery triennale, Sweden, Denmark, Norway, Finland

SEMINARS AND LECTURES
2009	'All about me', lecture at Pinakothek der Modern, München, Germany
2000	Speaker at 'A Sense of Wonder', Association for Contemporary Jewellery, Millenium Conference, Birmingham, UK

SELECTED PUBLICATIONS
2011	*Sigurd Bronger, Laboratorium Mechanum*, Arnoldsche Art publishing, Stuttgart, Germany

EDUCATION/TRAINING

1968–71	Postgraduate, Slade School of Fine Art, UCL, London, UK
1967	Postgraduate, Atelier 17, Paris, France
1963–67	Dip. A.D., Liverpool College of Art, UK

EMPLOYMENT/SELF-EMPLOYMENT

Self-employed

AWARDS

2008	Neuer Schmuck Preis, München, Germany
2005	Wingate Scholarship, London, UK
2003	Herbert Hofmann Preis, München, Germany
2000	Creative Scotland Award, Edinburgh, UK
1999	Inches Carr Trust Award, Edinburgh, UK
1995	Jerwood Prize for Jewellery, London, UK

COLLECTIONS

Alice & Louis Koch collection, Zurich, Switzerland
Contemporary Museum, Honolulu, Hawaii, USA
Danner-Stiftung, Die Neue Sammlung, Pinakothek der Moderne, München, Germany
Helsinki Museum of Art, Helsinki, Finland
Metropolitan Museum of Art, New York, USA
Musée des Arts Décoratifs, Montreal, Canada
Powerhouse Museum, Sydney, Australia
Royal Museums of Scotland, Edinburgh, UK
Schmuckmuseum, Pforzheim, Germany
Victoria and Albert Museum, London, UK

SOLO EXHIBITIONS

2007	Unnatural Selection, Walker Art Gallery, Liverpool, UK
2002–03	It's Only Plastic, Pforzheim, Berlin, München, Hanau and Idar-Oberstein, Germany
2003	Neue Arbeiten, Galerie Biro, München, Germany
2000	A Visionary, Taideteollisuusmuseo, Helsinki, Finland & American Crafts Museum, New York, USA
2000	Selected Works, Helen Drutt Gallery, Philadelphia, USA
1996	Schmucksachen 1980–96, Galerie Biro, München, Germany

1992	Peter Chang, Helen Drutt Gallery, Philadelphia, USA
1990	Peter Chang, Helen Drutt Gallery, New York, USA
1988	Peter Chang, Galerie RA, Amsterdam, Netherlands

GROUP EXHIBITIONS

2010	The Plastic Show, Velvet da Vinci, San Francisco, USA
2009	Design Miami, Ornamentum, Miami, USA
2008	Meister der Moderne, Internationalen Handwerkmesse, München, Germany
2006	Radiant, 30 Jaar Ra, Galerie RA, Amsterdam, Netherlands
2005	Lucca Preziosa, Villa Bottini, Lucca, Italy
2002	Zero Karat, American Crafts Museum, New York, USA
2001	Maskerade, Galerie RA, Amsterdam, Netherlands

SELECTED PUBLICATIONS

2007	Peter Chang, 'Unnatural Selection', A. Pollard, National Museums, Liverpool Ornament as Art, C. Strauss, Arnoldsche
2002	Peter Chang, Jewellery, Objects, Sculptures, C. Holzach, Arnoldsche
2000	Peter Chang, A Visionary, M. Aav & R. Hill

EDUCATION/TRAINING

1990–1992   Royal College of Art in London, Degree of Master of Arts in 1992
1985–1990   Pietro Selvatico High School of Art in Padova under the tuition of Francesco Pavan. During his school years at Pietro Selvatico, Giovanni worked in the workshops of Francesco Pavan and Paolo Maurizio

EMPLOYMENT/SELF-EMPLOYMENT

Self-employed

AWARDS

1998   Prize of the Unione Regionale delle Camere di Commercio dell'Umbria, Terni, Italy
1998   Highly Commended Work, International Jewellery Competition '97, Tokyo, Japan
1997   Bayerischer Staatspreis, München, Germany
1996   2nd Prize, Granulation '96, Pforzheim, Germany
1992   Herbert Hofmann Prize, München, Germany
1991   2nd Prize, Worshipful Company of Gold and Silver Wyre Drawers Competition, London, UK
1990   Maturità d'Arte Applicata
1988   Diploma di Maestro d'Arte

COLLECTIONS

2011   Nottingham Castle Museum and Art Gallery, UK
2010   The Alice and Louis Koch Collection of Rings, Switzerland
       Dallas Museum of Art, Dallas, USA
2009   MIMA (Middlesbrough Institute of Modern Art), Middlesbrough, UK
2008   The National Gallery of Australia, Canberra, Australia
       Museum of Arts and Design, New York, USA
2007   Museo degli Argenti e delle Porcellane, Palazzo Pitti, Firenze, Italy
2006   Schmuckmuseum, Pforzheim, Germany

SOLO EXHIBITIONS

2007   Gallery Katherine Kalaf, Perth, Australia
2006   Gallery Hipotésis, Barcelona, Spain
2004   Shedler Schmuck, Luzern, Switzerland

GROUP EXHIBITIONS

2011   Pavilion of Art & Design London 11, represented by Adrian Sassoon, London, UK
       Masterpiece, represented by Adrian Sassoon Gallery, London, UK
       Collect, Saatchi Gallery, represented by Clare Beck at Adrian Sassoon, London, UK
       TEFAF, represented by Adrian Sassoon Gallery, Maastricht, Netherlands
2010   Pavilion of Art & Design London 10, represented by Adrian Sassoon, London, UK
       Masterpiece, represented by Adrian Sassoon Gallery, London, UK
       Collect, Saatchi Gallery, represented by Clare Beck at Adrian Sassoon, London, UK
       Messe für Kunst und Antiquitäten Resedenz, Salzburg, represented by Spiegelgasse 8 Gallery, Salzburg, Austria
       TEFAF, represented by Adrian Sassoon Gallery, Maastricht, Netherlands
2009   Pavilion of Art & Design London, represented by Adrian Sassoon, London, UK
       Giovanni Corvaja: Alchemia, MIMA, Middlesbrough, UK
       Collect, Saatchi Gallery, represented by Clare Beck at Adrian Sassoon, London, UK
       The first public presentation of 'The Golden Fleece Collection', Meister Der Moderne, International Trade Fair, München, Germany

SELECTED PUBLICATIONS

Selected recent publications on the Golden Fleece Collection: *Edelmetaal*, The Netherlands, 2011
21st-century Jewelry The Best of the 500 Series, Marthe Le Van, Lark Books, USA, 2011
New Rings 500+ Designs From Around the World, Nicolas Estrada, Thames and Hudson, 2011
International Herald Tribune, The New York Times, 2011
Art Quarterly UK, 2010
Jewels Fashion Watches, UK, 2010
De Telegraaf, Netherlands, 2010
Apollo, The International Magazine for Collectors, 2010
International Herald Tribune, The New York Times, 2009
Vogue Joyas, Spain, 2009
The Jewelry, Korea, 2009

EDUCATION/TRAINING

2005–2010 Master of Arts Research, Fine Arts, Royal Melbourne Institute of Technology University (RMITU), Australia

1996–97 Honours, Fine Arts, RMITU, Melbourne, Australia

1994–96 BA Fine Arts, Gold and Silversmithing, RMITU, Melbourne, Australia

EMPLOYMENT/SELF-EMPLOYMENT

2009 Invited Visiting Artist Lecture, RMITU, Melbourne, Australia
Guest lecturer at South Carolina University Fine Arts, Greenville, USA; Massachusetts College of Fine Arts, Boston, USA

2008 Guest lecturer at State University of New York, New Paltz, USA
Guest lecturer at Rhode Island School of Art and Design, Providence, USA
Guest lecturer at Indiana University, Bloomington, USA
Guest lecturer at Pratt Institute, School of Art and Design, Brooklyn, NYC, USA
Guest lecturer at Auckland University, Manakau School of Visual Arts, New Zealand

2004–2007 Sessional lecturer in Fine Arts/Gold and Silversmithing, RMITU, Melbourne, Australia
Guest lecturer at LaSalle school of Fine Arts, Singapore

2002– Lecturer in fine arts/applied arts/metal, Monash University, Melbourne, Australia

1996–2008 Studio assistant to Robert Baines

1997 Assistant with large private commission to Frank Bauer, artist and metalsmith

1995, Nov–Dec Studio assistant to Mark Edgoose, artist and metalsmith

AWARDS

The National Contemporary Jewellery Award, Griffith Regional Art Gallery, Australia
Australia Council Grant, for personal study into creative intuition/ contemporary improvised music in NYC, USA
2nd prize, Refined Abundance International Art Jewellery Award, Opera House Art Centre, Texas, USA
RMITU Postgraduate Scholarship, Australia
Development Grant, Australia Council Visual Arts/Craft Fund
Peoples' Choice Award, Jewellers and Metalsmiths Group of Victoria, Australia

COLLECTIONS

Macmillan Collection, RMITU, Melbourne, Australia
Art Gallery of South Australia, Adelaide, Australia
National Gallery of Victoria, Melbourne, Australia
Espace Solidor, Ville de Cagnes-Sur-Mer, France

SOLO EXHIBITIONS

2003 Sound, Gallery Funaki, Melbourne, Australia

GROUP EXHIBITIONS

Over 80 group exhibitions since 1996 including;

2010 National Contemporary Jewellery Award Exhibition, Griffith Regional Art Gallery, Australia
By Example, Museum of Art/Craft, Itami, Japan
Schmuck, Internationale Handwerksmesse, München, Germany
Treasure Room Australia, Galerie Handwerk, München, Germany

2009 Four Jewellers: Baines/Bastin/Cottrell/ Haydon, Espace Solidor, Cagnes-Sur-Mer, France
Melbourne Hollow-ware, Galerie Marzee, Nijmegen, Netherlands

2008 SOFA Chicago, Navy Pier, Chiagao, USA (presented by Charon Kransen Arts)
Schmuck, Internationale Handwerksmesse, München, Germany
The Rhianon Vernon-Roberts Memorial Collection, Art Gallery of South Australia, Adelaide, Australia

2006 Connect, Inaugural Gallery Funaki International Contemporary Jewellery Prize
Colin and Cicely Rigg Contemporary Design Award, National Gallery of Victoria, Melbourne, Australia

2005 Space, Place and Proximity, Elaine Jacob Gallery, Detroit, Michigan, USA
10-2005, Tenth anniversary exhibition, Gallery Funaki, Melbourne, Australia

EDUCATION/TRAINING

2001–2003	MA Goldsmithing, Silversmithing, Metalwork & Jewellery, Royal College of Art, London, UK
2000	April–July, study exchange program in Fachhochshule Trie in Idar-Obarstein, Germany
1998–2001	BA (hons) Silversmithing, Goldsmithing and Jewellery Design, Kent Institute of Art and Design, Rochester, Kent, UK

EMPLOYMENT/SELF-EMPLOYMENT

2004–2009	Artist in Residence, School of Jewellery, Birmingham City University, UK
1991–1998	Full-time packaging designer at Alfa Box, Osaka, Japan
1985–1989	PA for director at the Osaka division of synthetic reins at C. Itoh Co. Ltd., Osaka, Japan

AWARDS

2007	Grants for the arts by Arts Council West Midlands, UK
	Finalist in Jerwood Applied Arts Prize 2007: Jewellery, UK
2004	Chelsea Crafts Fair 'First Time Exhibitors Award'
2003	Itami International Craft Competition – Jewellery 'Good Material Award'
	Nicole Stöber Memorial Award
	Goldsmiths' Craft and Design Council Craftsmanship and Design Award
	Commended, Fashion Jewellers Finished Pieces

COLLECTIONS

2008	Crafts Council (a group of wrapped objects)
2005	Aberdeen Art Gallery and Museums (neckpiece)
2003	Royal College of Art (clear sphere necklace & veiled ring)
2003	Alice and Louis Koch Collection (veiled ring)

SOLO EXHIBITION

2007	Gallery CAJ, Kyoto, Japan

GROUP EXHIBITIONS

2010	Material versus Form, Galleria Cristiani, Torino, Italy
	New York International Gift Fair, Jacob Javits Convention Center, New York, USA
	Contemporary Jewellery exhibition, Gallery Tougendo, Japan
	Blumenwiese, Galerie Cebra, Dusseldorf, Germany
	Across borders, Studio Gabi Green, München, Germany
2009	Wrapped Up, Devon Guild of Craftsmen, Bovey Tracey, UK
	Material versus Form, Galleria Cristiani, Torino, Italy
	La Crème, Lesley Craze Gallery, London, UK
	Sieraad 2009, Cultural Park Westergasfabrik, Amsterdam, Netherlands
	What's New, Galerie Sofie Lachaert, Tielrode, Belgium
	Three by One, Crafts Study Centre, University for the Creative Arts, Farnham, UK
	Show Case, Stroud International Textile Festival, Stroud, UK
2008	Ring, Gallery CAJ, Kyoto, Japan
	Show Case, The Scottish Gallery, Edinburgh, UK
	Show Case, Yorkshire Sculpture Park, Wakefield, UK
	Contemporary Japanese Jewelry, Keiko Gallery, Boston, USA
	SOFA, represented by The David Collection, New York, USA
	Masters and Protégés – Contemporary British Jewellery, The Museum of Arts Crafts Itami, Japan
	Schmuck 2008, Handwerksmesse, München, Germany
	Korean & Japanese Jewellery, Gana Art Gallery, Seoul, South Korea
	Collect, represented by Lesley Craze Gallery, Victoria and Albert Museum, London, UK

SELECTED PUBLICATIONS

Dreaming Jewelry, Miquela Abellan, 2010, Monsa
Adorn – New Jewellery, Amanda Mansell, 2008, Laurence King Publishing Ltd.
Jewellery Design, 2008, DAAB
USE fashion journal (Brazil), No.68 Sep 2009
Selvedge, Sep/Oct 19 issue 08

SOLO EXHIBITIONS

2006	Still, Object Gallery, Sydney, Australia
2005	Hnoss, Sweden
	V&V Vienna, Austria, & Spectrum München, Germany (travelling)
2004	Hélène Porée Gallery, Paris, France

GROUP EXHIBITIONS

2010	Un peu de terre sur la peau, Foundation Bernardaud, France
2009	NY NY: Right Before My Eyes, Gallery Loupe, USA
	Glasswear, Museum of Arts and Design, NY, USA
	Inspired Jewelry, Museum of Arts and Design, NY, USA
2008	Glasswear, Toledo Museum of Arts, USA
	Just Must, Estonian History Museum, Estonia
	From Hand to Hand, Mudac Museum, Lausanne, Switzerland
2007	Vaar Wel, Gallery RA, Amsterdam, Netherlands
	Collect, Craft Council fair, Victoria and Albert Museum, London, UK
2006	Radiant 30 Years, Gallery RA, Netherlands
	Women in Jewellery, Alternatives Gallery, Roma, Italy
	Collect, Craft Council fair, London, UK
2004	Influence, National Museum of Ireland, Dublin, Ireland
	Qua Art, Beeld en Aambeeld, Netherlands
2003	Euromix, Kath Libbert Gallery, UK
	Schmuck, München, Germany
2002	Sieraden nu, Textielmuseum, Netherlands
	Zonder wrijving geen glans, Centraal Museum Utrecht, Netherlands
	Dutch Design Events, Foreign affairs/ Kransen New York, USA

COMMISSIONS, ACTIVITIES

2006	EKWC, Netherlands, artist in residence
2005	Idar-Oberstein, Germany, Turnov Symposium artist in residence
2004	Wien, Austria, artist in residence
2003	Tijd voor sieraad, Netherlands

2002	Kunstuitleen Zwolle, Netherlands, multiple
2001	Haags Gemeente Museum, Netherlands, exclusive series for museum shop
1992	Ministry of Culture of the Netherlands
1993	Forum für Schmuck, Germany, multiple
1994	Threes Moolhuysen, Netherlands, multiple
1995	Voorzieningsfonds voor Kunstenaars, Netherlands, award and multiple: Estafettestokje

WORKSHOPS, SEMINARS AND LECTURES

2009	Massart Boston, USA, workshop & lecture
2008	Cranbrook School of Arts, USA, lecture & student talks
	92 Y, USA, workshop
2006	JMGA Conference, Sydney, Australia, lecture, workshop & residency
2004	Ortweinschule Graz, Austria, lecture
	Academy of Fine Arts Bratislava, Slovakia, lecture
	Stoss am Himmel, Austria, lecture
2002	School of Jewellery UCE Birmingham, UK, guest teacher
2001	SHKS Oslo, Norway, guest teacher
	HEAA Geneva Bijou et Objet, Switzerland, lecture

SELECTED PUBLICATIONS

Un peu de terre sur la peau, France, 2010
Compendium, Germany, 2009
From Hand to Hand, Switzerland, 2008
Art Jewelry Today, USA, 2008
Just Must, Estonia, 2008
Herinner-ring-remember, Netherlands, 2008
Hnoss Dependend, Sweden, 2007
Glasswear, USA, 2007
Alternatives gallery 'Collect', Italy, 2006–7
Radiant, Netherlands, 2006
Plus 5, Germany, 2006
Schmuck magazine article, Germany, 2006
Wanderungen Rian de Jong, Germany, 2005
500 Brooches, USA, 2005
Verbeelding van verlangen, Netherlands, 2004
Influence, Ireland, 2004
1000 Rings, USA, 2004

EDUCATION/TRAINING

2006–2007   Master of Arts, Jewellery, Silversmithing and Related Products, BCU, Birmingham Institute of Art and Design, Birmingham, UK. Distinction.

2006   Gesellenprüfung, Goldschmied in Idar-Oberstein, Germany (Goldsmith Apprenticeship Exam in Idar-Oberstein, Germany)

2005–2006   BA (Hons), Jewellery and Silversmithing, BCU, Birmingham Institute of Art and Design, Birmingham, UK. First Class Honours.

2003–2005   Prediploma (Vordiplom), University of Applied Gemstone and Jewellery Design, Idar-Oberstein, Germany

EMPLOYMENT/SELF-EMPLOYMENT

2007–   Course Director of Jewellery Foundation Course at AIVA, Academy of International Visual Arts, Shanghai, China

EXHIBITIONS

2010/2011   BKV-Prize Finalist with exhibition at the Bayerische Kunstgewerbeverein, Kunstmesse München and the 63 Internationale Handwerksmesse, München, Germany

2010   Into Flora group exhibition at Kath Libbert Jewellery Gallery, Salts Mill, UK
Finger Symbols, Shetland Arts, Toll Clock Centre, Shetland
Bluehende Fantasien group exhibition at Gallery craft2eu, Hamburg, Germany
TALENTE Sonderschau der Internationalen Handwerksmesse, München, Germany
Dear JAMES, Atelier Klarastrasse, München, Germany

2009/2010   Brilliantly Birmingham Retrospective, Museum and Art Gallery, Birmingham, UK
BKV-Prize finalist with exhibition at Bayerische Kunstgewerbeverein, Kunstmesse München and the 62 Internationale Handwerksmesse, München, Germany

2009   Wearable Art and Non-Functional Jewellery, Two Cities Gallery, Shanghai, China
SOFA West USA; SOFA New York, USA; SOFA Chicago, USA, all represented by Charon Kransen Arts
The JAMES Exchange, Atelier Klarastrasse, München, Germany

2008/2009   BKV-Prize Finalist with exhibition at Bayerische Kunstgewerbeverein, Kunstmesse München and the 61 Internationale Handwerksmesse, München, Germany

2008   Non-Craftsman, Nooca, Nanjing, China
Project/Product, jewellery exhibition at 18K Gold Tone, Portland, Oregon, USA
Masters and Protegés, Itami and Tokyo, Japan
Beauty of the Lost, contemporary jewellery and art exhibition at Gallery Star Space, Shanghai, China
JAMES on stage, Atelier Klarastrasse, München, Germany
Design City, Birmingham, UK

2007   Brilliantly Birmingham 2007, Museum and Art Gallery, Birmingham, UK
First Prize at Louisa Anne Ryland Competition, Birmingham Institute of Art and Design, UK

SELECTED PUBLICATIONS

2010   *West East* Magazine, Issue 30, 'Ode to Jewellers', Hong Kong, China
Art Aurea, March 2010, Talente

2009   *The Compendium Finale of Contemporary Jewellery Makers*, Darling Publications, Cologne, Germany
ICS, City Beat TV Show, 10 Feb, Shanghai, China
Ornament Magazine, Volume 33, No.1

2008   *Self* Magazine, Nov, 'Learn around the World', Shanghai, China
Life Element Magazine, September, issue 94, 'World of Contemporary Jewellery', Hong Kong, China

EDUCATION/TRAINING

1994	Complementary studies at Bernd Munsteiner lapidary studio, Germany
1993–94	Studies on gemmology by Esko Timonen, Lahti Design Institute, Finland
1986	Graduated from the Estonian Academy of Arts by Prof Kuldkepp

EMPLOYMENT/SELF-EMPLOYMENT

1996–	Professor of Jewellery
1995–1996	Head of Jewellery and Blacksmithing Department
1989–1995	Assignment at the Estonian Academy of Arts
1986–	Freelance artist

AWARDS

2010	Tanel Veenre Orden, Estonia
2005	GRAND PRIX of the 2nd European Triennial of Contemporary Jewellery, Belgium
2004	Ted Noten Gold Prize, Amsterdam, Netherlands
2003	Ordem do Mérito of the Republic of Portugal
	Estonian National Library, annual prize for best artbook (teamwork)
2001	Ars Ornata Heart Award, Germany
1998	Estonian State Culture Award
1997	Annual Prize of Cultural Endowment, Estonia
	Award of Excellence, Tenth Cloisonne Jewellery Contest, Tokyo, Japan
1994	Kristjan Raud Award (Artist of the Year), Estonia
1992	PRIX ARCTICA Honourable Mention, Finland
1988	GRAND PRIX of the IV Baltic Applied Art Triennial, Estonia
1987	Young Artists' Annual Prize, Estonia

COLLECTIONS

Museum of Applied Art and Design, Estonia
Museum of Decorative and Applied Arts, Moscow, Russia
Tallinn Art Hall Collection, Estonia
Royal College of Art, London, UK
KunstgewerbeMuseum, Berlin, Germany
Museum für Kunst und Gerwerbe, Hamburg, Germany
Victoria and Albert Museum, London, UK
Fine Art Museum, Houston, USA
Espace Solidor Collection, Cagnes-sur-Mer, France
The Alice and Louis Koch Collection, Switzerland
The Helen Drutt Collection, USA
The Pahlman Collection, Finland
The Bollmann Collection, Wien, Austria

SOLO EXHIBITIONS

2010	Dominican Monastery, Tallinn, Estonia
2007	Espace Solidor, Cagnes-sur-Mer, France (with Piret Hirv and Tanel Veenre)
2007	Galerie Biró, München, Germany (with Piret Hirv and Tanel Veenre)
2004	Galeria Reverso, Lisboa, Portugal
2003	Galeria Shibuichi, Porto, Portugal
2002	Galerii Hnoss, Konstepidemin, Gothenburg, Sweden
2000/01	Museum of Applied Art, Tallinn, Estonia
1998	Galerie Biró, München, Germany
1997	Rotermann Salt Storage, Tallinn, Estonia
1996	Galerie Farel, Aigle, Switzerland
1995	Galerie Néon, Bruxelles, Belgium
1994	Saaremaa Museum, Kuressaare Castle, Estonia
1993	Luum Gallery, Tallinn, Estonia
1991	Gallery of Applied Art Center Verkaranta, Tampere, Finland

GROUP EXHIBITIONS

Numerous participations in group exhibitions in Estonia, the Netherlands, Spain, Germany, Denmark, Portugal, Hungary, Bulgaria, Poland, Czech Republic, Slovakia, Latvia, Lithuania, UK, Finland, Norway, Sweden, Belgium, Italy, Greece, France, Switzerland, Austria, Australia, Korea, Japan, USA and China

PUBLICATIONS

Author and publisher of books and texts on jewellery art, including the personal collection Kadri Mälk (2001), a volume accompanying the international jewellery exhibition Just Must (2008), jewellery group Castle in the Air (2011)

EDUCATION/TRAINING

1985–88	Printmaking and Etching, Chelsea School of Art, London, UK
1980–83	MA, Royal College of Art, London, UK
1975–80	Diploma/Post-Diploma in Art, Duncan of Jordanstone College of Art, Dundee, UK

EMPLOYMENT/SELF-EMPLOYMENT

2001–	Part-time Lecturer, Massana School of Art, Barcelona, Spain
2005–07	Visiting Lecturer, Edinburgh College of Art, Edinburgh, UK
2005	Filigree Symposium, Travassos, Portugal
2005	Amber Symposium, Gdansk, Poland
2004	Visiting Lecturer, ESAD School of Art, Porto, Portugal
2003	Symposium, Peter's Valley Centre, New Jersey, USA
2003	Visiting Lecturer, Syracuse University, USA
2002	Symposium, Turnov, Czech Republic

AWARDS

2010	Grand Prix, joint first prize, Minimum, 19th Legnica International Jewellery Competition, Galerie Sztuki w Legnicy, Legnica, Poland
2005	The Amber Competition 'Alatyr', Russia
1989	Greater London Arts Grant for Individual Artists, UK
1987	Crafts Council Setting Up Grant-Established Studio in London, UK

COLLECTIONS

Crafts Council Collection, London, UK
Scottish Crafts Council/National Museums of Scotland, Edinburgh, UK
Medal commissioned by British Art Medal Society, British Museum, London, UK
Vydalo Museum, Ceskeho ráje, Turnov, Czech Republic
Elizabeth Moignard Private Collection, Glasgow, UK

SOLO EXHIBITIONS

2010	Through Night and Day, The Scottish Gallery, Edinburgh, UK
2009	A Través de las Nubes Blancas, Amaranto Gallery, Barcelona, Spain
2007	Between Sky and Earth, Queen's Hall Arts Centre, Hexham, Northumberland, UK
2006	Across Unnamed Seas, Al '65', Vilanova i la Geltrú, Spain
2005	Wandering Earth, The Scottish Gallery, Edinburgh, UK
2003	Between Worlds, Hipótesi, Barcelona, Spain

GROUP EXHIBITIONS

2010	Pezzi Di Luna 2, Music and Contemporary Jewellery, Cultural Centre, Maribor, Slovenia
2010	Connexions/Transversals, professors from The Massana School, Gallery Amaranto, Barcelona, Spain
2010	True Colours, New Traditional Jewellery, Sieraad Fair, Amsterdam and travelling
2010	Premio Fondazione Cominelli, Salò, Lake Garda, Italy
2010	Minimum, 19th Legnica International Jewellery Competition, The Gallery of Art, Legnica, Poland
2009/10	Paradigma, work by staff at Birmingham City University/Massana School, Barcelona, Spain
2005/7/8	A Hundred Brooch/Earring/ Pendant Show, Velvet da Vinci Gallery, San Francisco, USA
2008	Collect, The Scottish Gallery, Victoria and Albert Museum, London, UK
2007	Schmuck 2007, München, Germany / Oratorio di San Rocco, Padova, Italy
2005	Maker, Wearer, Viewer, Narrative Jewellery, GSA, Glasgow, UK/The Scottish Gallery, UK/Galerie Marzee, Netherlands

PUBLICATIONS

Adorn: New Jewellery, Amanda Mansell
500 Brooches, Lark Books, 2005
500 Pendants, Lark Books
Shining Through, Crafts Council and Marina Vaizey, 1995
Catalogue *Jewellery Moves,* NMS publishing
International Craft, Martina Margetts, Thames & Hudson Ltd. London, 1991
Crafts Magazine, UK

RUUDT PETERS

EDUCATION/TRAINING

1970–1974   Studied Jewellery design at Gerrit Rietveld
              Academie, Amsterdam, Netherlands
1967–1970   Studied Medical Instrumentmaking at
              Fysiological Labor, Leiden, Netherlands

EMPLOYMENT/SELF-EMPLOYMENT

1974–   Self-employed visual artist

AWARDS

2005   Marzee Award, Gallery Marzee, Nijmegen,
              Netherlands
2004   Herbert Hofmann Award 2004 (for Iosis)
              München, Germany
2000   Françoise van den Bosch Award 2000 (for
              oeuvere), Amsterdam, Netherlands

COLLECTIONS

2008   Racine Art Museum, Wisconsin, USA
              Metropolitan Museum of Art, New York,
              USA
2007   Museum Catharijneconvent, Utrecht,
              Netherlands
              Schmuck Museum, Pforzheim, Germany
              Alice and Louis Koch Collection,
              Switzerland
              Mint Museum Craft & Design, Charlotte,
              USA
2006   Museum of Art and Design (MAD), New
              York, USA
              Mint Museum Craft & Design, Charlotte,
              USA
2005   Houston Museum, Houston, USA
2004   Staatliches Museum für angewandte
              Kunst Design in Pinakothek der Moderne,
              München (on permanent loan from the
              Danner Foundation, München, Germany)
2003   Museum für Kunst und Gewerbe, Hamburg,
              Germany
              Amsterdams Historisch Museum,
              Netherlands

SOLO EXHIBITIONS

2011   Anima, Galerie Spektrum, München,
              Germany

2010   Introduction, Galerie Rob Koudijs,
              Amsterdam, Netherlands
              Anima, Art Basel Design, Galerie Caroline
              van Hoek, Switzerland
              Anima, SOFA NY by Ornamentum Hudson,
              USA
              Anima, Galerie Marzee, Nijmegen,
              Netherlands
              Lingam, Galerie Caroline van Hoek,
              Bruxelles, Belgium
2008   Lingam, Galerie Phoebus, Rotterdam,
              Netherlands
2007   Sefiroth, Ornamentum Hudson, New York,
              USA

GROUP EXHIBITIONS

Various shows around the world

SELECTED PUBLICATIONS

2006   *Sefiroth*, text by Jorunn Veiteberg
2002   *Change*, text by Liesbeth den Besten, Marie
              Jose van den Hout, Rob Kurvers
2000   *Pneuma*, text by Gabi Dewald
1997   *Lapis*, text by Gert Staal
1995   *Ouroboros*, text by Jan Hein Sassen
1992   *Passio*, text by Marjan Unger
1991   *Interno*, text by Ans van Berkum

NATALYA PINCHUK

EDUCATION/TRAINING

2005	MFA, University of Illinois, Urbana-Champaign, USA
2001	BFA, Indiana University, Bloomington, USA

EMPLOYMENT/SELF EMPLOYMENT

2007–2010	Assistant Professor, School of the Arts, Craft/Material Studies Department, Virginia Commonwealth University, Richmond, USA
2005–2007	Assistant Professor, Head of Art Metal Jewelry Program, School of Art, Stephen F. Austin State University, Nacogdoches, USA

AWARDS

2010	Virginia Museum of Fine Arts Fellowship, professional category, USA
2008	Louis Comfort Tiffany Foundation Award, Nominee, USA
2006	AJF Winner, Art Jewelry Forum Emerging Artist Award Competition, USA
	AVP Support Fund, Stephen F. Austin State University, USA
	Professional Development Grant, Fine Arts Council, Stephen F. Austin State University, USA
	School of Art Faculty Development Grant, Stephen F. Austin State University, USA

COLLECTIONS

2008	Stedelijk Museum, Hertogenbosch, Netherlands
2006	Mint Museum of Craft and Design, Charlotte, USA

SOLO AND TWO-PERSON EXHIBITIONS

2009	Yes, We are Jewelers... Yes, We are Sisters... Jewelers' Werk Galerie, Washington, USA
2008	Growth Series Galerie Rob Koudijs, Amsterdam, Netherlands

GROUP EXHIBITIONS

2010	Plastic Show, Velvet da Vinci Gallery, San Francisco, USA
	20/20, School of Art + Design Gallery, University of Illinois, Urbana-Champaign, USA
	IntoFlora, Kath Libbert Jewellery Gallery, Bradford, UK
	SOFA Chicago, SOFA NY, USA, represented by Charon Kransen Arts
	Schmuck 2010, 62nd International Trade Fair, München, Germany
	Transmutations: Material Reborn (travelling)
	Not the Family Jewels, Gallery 1724, Houston, USA
	Ugly Objects, Centrale Bibliotheek, Amsterdam, Netherlands
	10th International Shoebox Sculpture Exhibition (travelling)
2009	Garbage Pin Project (travelling)
	The Stimulus Project, Sienna Gallery, Lenox, USA (invitational)
	The Enamel Show, Velvet da Vinci, San Francisco, USA (invitational)
	Collect with Rob Koudijs Galerie, Saatchi Gallery, London, UK
	Crossing the Border, exhibition with Jang-shin-gu-sang/Jewelry Conception (invitational, travelling)
	SOFA Chicago, SOFA NY, USA, represented by Charon Kransen Arts
	Object Rotterdam with Rob Koudijs Galerie, Rotterdam, Netherlands
	The New Iconoclasts, Hoffman Gallery, Oregon College of Art and Craft, Portland, USA (invitational)
	Garbage Pin Project (travelling)
	10th International Shoebox Sculpture Exhibition (travelling)

PUBLICATIONS

Textile Plus, Netherlands, Nov. 2009 (article with images)

Perkins, S. *500 Enameled Objects*, New York: Lark Books, 2009 (images)

Keah, S. *Jewellery Using Textile Techniques*, London: A&C Black, 2009 (images, text)

Mansell, A. *Adorn*, London: Laurence King, 2008 (images)

Haywood, J. *Mixed Media Jewellery*, London: A&C Black, 2009 (images)

Legg, B. *Jewellery from Natural Materials,* London: A&C Black, 2008 (images)

PETER SKUBIC

EDUCATION/TRAINING
Akademie für Angewandte Kunst, Wien, Austria

EMPLOYMENT/SELF EMPLOYMENT
Professor at Fachhochschule, Köln, Germany
Guest professor at Burg Giebichenstein, Hochschule für
Kunst und Design, Halle / Saale Professor at Sommer-
Akademie, Salzburg, Austria

AWARDS
Ehrenring der Gesellschaft für Goldschmiedekunst
Bayerischer Staatspreis, Germany
Preis der Stadt, Wien, Austria

COLLECTIONS
Metropolitan Museum, New York, USA
Museum of Modern Art, Kyoto, Japan
Museum of Arts and Design, New York, USA
Museum Ludwig, Aachen, Germany
Collection Asenbaum, Wien, Austria
Collection Bollmann, Klosterneuburg, Austria
Die Neue Sammlung, München, Germany
Museum 20. Jahrhundert, Wien, Austria

SOLO EXHIBITIONS
Lo Speccio Della Creativita, Oratorio di San Rocco, Padova,
Italy
Wallpieces-Spacepieces, Galerie Arcis, Sarvar, Ungarn,
South Korea
Peter Skubic, Künstlerhaus, Wien, Austria
Museum 20. Jahrhundert, Wien, Austria
Wandstücke, Galerie Chobot, Wien, Austria
Spannung.Spiegelung, Galerie Marktschlösschen, Halle/
Saale, Germany
Schmuck aus 30 Jahren, Galerie für Angewandte Kunst
BKV, München, Germany
Museum 20. Jahrhundert, Wien, Austria
Spiegelverkehrt, Kunsthalle Krems, Austria
Peter Skubic, Galerie Louise Smit, Amsterdam, Netherlands
Between, Schmuckmuseum Pforzheim, Germany
Unsichtbar, Galerie Spektrum, München, Germany
Der Kosmos des Peter Skubic, Grassi-Museum, Leipzig and
Museum für Angewandte Kunst, Köln, Germany
Without Guarantee, Galerie Spektrum, München, Germany
Halbzeit, Galerie am Graben, Wien, Austria

GROUP EXHIBITIONS
10 Jahre Galerie 422, Gmunden, Austria
Ornament as Art – The Helen Drutt Collection, Museum of
Fine Art, Houston, USA
Wearables, Alles Schmuck, Sammlung Inge Asenbaum,
Museum für Gesteltung, Zürich, Switzerland
Kunst hautnah, Künstlerhaus, Wien, Austria
Mikromegas, Bayerischer Kunstverein BVK, München,
Germany
Radiant Geometries, American Craft Museum, New York,
USA
Joias de Amigos, Galleria Contacto Directo, Lisboa, Portugal
Facet I, Kunsthal, Rotterdam, Netherlands
Tragezeichen, Museum Morsbroich, Leverkusen, Germany

SELECTED PUBLICATIONS
Katalog Peter Skubic 'lo specchio della creativita'
Katalog Peter Skubic, 'Between'
Katalog Peter Skubic, 'Spiegelverkehrt
Katalog Peter Skubic, 'der Kosmos des Peter Skubic'
Katalog Peter Skubic 'Halbzeit'
Katalog Peter Skubic 'Skubic – Schmuck und Objekte'

GRAZIANO VISINTIN

EDUCATION/TRAINING
Graduated from Pietro Selvatico Art Institute, Padova, Italy

EMPLOYMENT/SELF-EMPLOYMENT
Teacher at Pietro Selvatico Art Institute, Padova, since 1976
Lives and works in Padova, Italy

AWARDS

2009	Master Prize European Prize for Applied Arts, World Craft Council Belgique Francophone, Mons, Belgium
1990	Bayerischer Staatspreis, Goldmedaille, München, Germany
	Honourable Mention 'Signaturen', Schwabisch Gmund, Germany
1988	Herbert Hofmann Preis, Schmuckszene 88, München, Germany
	3 Preis 'Art & Design', Benson & Hedges Gold, Hamburg, Germany

COLLECTIONS
Collection Marzee, Nijmegen, Netherlands
Die Neue Sammlung, Staatliches Museum für Angewangte Kunst, Design in der Pinakothek der Moderne, Dauerleihgabe der Danner-Stiftung, München, Germany
Hiko Mizuno College, Tokyo, Japan
Inge Asembaum, Wien, Austria
Landesmuseum Joanneum, Graz, Austria
Musée des Arts Décoratifs, Palais du Louvre, Paris, France
Schmuckmuseum, Pforzheim, Germany
Studio GR 20, Padova, Italy
Victoria and Albert Museum, London, UK

SOLO EXHIBITIONS

2011	Alternatives Gallery, Roma, Italy
2004	Galerie Marzee, Nijmegen, Netherlands
1998	Galerie Hélène Porée, Paris, France
	Galerie Marzee, Nijmegen, Netherlands

GROUP EXHIBITIONS

2011	Schmuck 2011, IHM, München, Germany
	Collect – Saatchi Gallery, London, UK
2010	Lingam, Museum Catharijneconvent, Utrecht, Netherlands
	Vita Havet Gallery, Konstfack-Hagersten, Stockholm, Sweden
	Meister der Moderne 62° Internationalen Handwerksmesse, München, Germany
	Bijoux – Precious Design – Pierre Bergé, Salle des Beaux-Arts, Bruxelles, Belgium
	Gioiello Contemporaneo Due, Palazzo Pitti, Firenze, Italy
	Unique Arts and Crafts-Messe, Karlsruhe, Germany
	Premio per il Gioiello Contemporaneo, Fondazione Cominelli, Cisano s/B Brescia, Italy
	Collect, Saatchi Gallery, London, UK
	Pezzi di Luna, Betnava Mansion, Maribor, Slovenia
	Art Meets Jewellery – 20 Jahre, Galerie Slavik, Wien, Austria
2009	Cutting the Mirror, Lucca Preziosa, Villa Bottini, Lucca, Italy
	Frame, Galerie GR20 München, Germany
	Gioielli d'Autore, Padova e la Scuola dell'Oro, Handwerk Galerie, München, Germany
	Collect, Saatchi Gallery, London, UK
	European Prize for Applied Arts, World Craft Council Belgique Francophone, Mons, Belgium

WORKSHOPS AND LECTURES

2009	Lecture, Lucca Preziosa, Villa Bottini, Lucca, Italy
	Workshop, Museum Casalmaggiore, Cremona, Italy
2007	Herbert Hofmann Preis, München, Germany
	Lecture, SOFA, Chicago, USA

BIBLIOGRAPHY

2010	*Prix Européen des Arts Appliqués*, World Craft Council Belgique Francophone, Mons, Belgium
2009	M.C. Bergesio, (a cura di) *Cutting the Mirror*, Le Arti Orafe-Jewellery School, Firenze, Italy
2008	A. Cappellieri, Gioiello Italiano *Contemporaneo-Tecniche e materiali tra Arte e Design*, SKIRA Milano, Italy

MIZUKO YAMADA

EDUCATION/TRAINING

1990–91   Research student, Tankin Department, Tokyo University of Fine Art and Music

1990   Graduated Tokyo University of Fine Arts and Music, Masters Course in Tankin Department of Craft

1988   Graduated Tokyo University of Fine Arts and Music, Bachelor of Arts in Choukin Department of Craft

EMPLOYMENT/SELF-EMPLOYMENT

2007–   Part-time lecturer at Aoyama University, Girls' Junior College department, Tokyo

2005–   Part-time lecturer at Tama Art College, Tokyo Promote Choukin and Jewellery Course

2003–8   Intensive course 'Introduction to Jewellery' and Workshop lecturer at Glasshouse, Tokyo, Japan

2002–5   Part-time lecturer at Atomi Girls' College, Junior College department, Tokyo, Japan

2000–7   Part-time lecturer at Hiko Mizuno Jewellery College, Tokyo, Japan

1999–   Lecturer at Asahi Culture Center, Jewellery-Making Course, Tokyo, Japan

1996–2000   Part-time lecturer at Touhoku University of Art and Technology, Yamagata, Japan

1996–   Part-time lecturer at Tokyo Metropolitan High School of Craft, Tokyo, Japan

AWARDS

2010   Grand Prize, Japan Jewellery Art Competition by Japan Jewellery Designers Association

2009   Tansuiou Prize from Satoh Foundation

1996   Encouragement prize in Takaoka Craft Competition

1990   Harada Prize for MA graduation work

COLLECTIONS

2005   Tactile Ring for a Wearer, Tactile Ring, Powerhouse Museum, Sydney, Australia

2003   Rings, Hiko-Mizuno Jewelery College, Tokyo Pin, Die Neue Sammlung, Staatliches Museum für angewandte Kunst, Design in Pinakothek der Moderne, on permanent loan from the Danner Foundation, München, Germany

1998   Pair of Earrings, Hiko-Mizuno Jewellery College, Tokyo, Japan

1995   Mokume Box, Royal College of Art, London, UK

SOLO EXHIBITIONS

2010   Torindo, Tokyo, Japan

2009   Gallery Shimon, Yokohama, Japan
Dan-Ginza, Tokyo, Japan
Mobilia Gallery, Boston, USA

2008   Gallery Yori, Tokyo, Japan

2007   Torindo, Tokyo, Japan
Seikado, Kyoto, Japan

2006   Gallery Tonan, Toyama
Arai Atelier Gallery, Tokyo, Japan

2005   Gallery Yori, Tokyo, Japan

2004   Torindo, Tokyo, Japan

2003   Arai Atelier Gallery, Tokyo, Japan

2002   Gallery Yori, Tokyo, Japan

2001   West Village, Kyushu, Japan
Torindo, Tokyo, Japan

GROUP EXHIBITIONS

2010   Show with Hokuto Ito at Mitsukoshi department store art gallery (2008, 2006)

2009   Cheongju International Craft Biennale

2009   Dissolving Views, South Korea
Inner Vision at Contemporary Applied Art, London, UK
Collect from Gallery Flow, Saatchi gallery, London, UK

2008   Transition, Bilston Craft Gallery, UK, touring to New Brewery Arts Centre, Doncaster Museum and Art Gallery, UK

2006   Transfiguration: Japanese Art Jewelry Today, Tokyo National Museum of Modern Art Craft Gallery, Japan

2005   Contemporary Japanese Jewellery, Object Gallery, Sydney, Australia

BIBLIOGRAPHY

Anon. (1990) *Sweat of the Sun: Gold of Peru*. Edinburgh: City of Edinburgh Museums and Art Galleries.

Baal-Teshuva, J. (2002) Alexander Calder. Köln: Taschen.

Barros, A. (1997) *Ornament and Object: Canadian Jewelry and Metal Art*. Toronto: Boston-Mills Press.

Bernabei, R. (2011) *Contemporary Jewellers*. Oxford: Berg.

Bloxham, J. ed. (2007) *Romancing the Stone*. Manchester: Ars Ornata Europeana.

Cartlidge, B. (1985) *Twentieth-Century Jewellery*. New York: H. N. Abrams.

Cellini, B. (1961) Autobiography. New York: Dodd, Mead.

Costello, D. and Vickery, J. eds. (2007) *Art: Key Contemporary Thinkers*. Oxford: Berg.

Danto, A. (1997) *After the End of Art*. Princeton: Princeton University Press.

Dormer, P. ed. (1997) *The Culture of Craft*. Manchester: Manchester University Press.

Drutt, H. and Dormer, P. (1995) *Jewelry of Our Time: Art, Ornament and Obsession*. London: Thames and Hudson.

Estrada, N. (2011), *New Rings*. London: Thames and Hudson.

Falk, F. (1993) *Treasures from the Pforzheim Collection*. London: The Worshipful Company of Goldsmiths.

Frayling, C. (2011) *On Craftsmanship*. London: Oberon Books.

Grant, C. ed. (2005). *New Directions in Jewellery*. London: Black Dog Publishing.

Hufnagel, F. ed. (1997) *Plastics*. Stuttgart: Arnoldsche.

Hughes, G. (1984) *The Art of Jewellery*. New York: Studio Vista.

Lawson, B. (2006) *How Designers Think: The Design Process Demystified*. Oxford: The Architectural Press.

Lignel, B. and Veiteberg, J. eds. (2009) *'Speed'. Think Tank, a European Initiative for the Applied Arts*.

Lindemann, W. ed. (2011) *Thinking Jewellery: On the Way Towards a Theory of Jewellery*. Stuttgart: Arnoldsche.

Lohmann, J. and Funder, L. eds. (1995) *Nordic Jewellery*. Copenhagen: Nyt Nordisk Forlag.

Martin, L. (2006) *Beyond Material, Innovative Jewellery and Design*. Delft: Louis Martin/Stichting Sieraad en Vormgeving.

Maxwell-Hyslop, K. R. (1971) *Western Asiatic Jewellery*. London: Methuen.

Moolhuysen-Coenders, T. ed. (2001) Onedel: Nonprecious. *Schiedam: Stichting Tekens en Tekens*.

Peters, R. and van den Hout, G. eds. (2010) *Lingam*. Stuttgart: Arnoldsche.

Petroski, H. (1994) *The Evolution of Useful Things*. New York: Vintage Books.

Rosa, J. (2006) *Xefirotarch*. San Francisco: San Francisco Museum of Modern Art.

Schadt, H. (1996) *Goldsmiths' Art: 5000 Years of Jewelry and Hollowware*. Stuttgart, Arnoldsche.

Tait, H. (1978) *Jewellery through 7000 Years*. London: British Museum Publications.

Turner, R. (1996) *Jewelry in Europe and America: New Times, New Thinking*. London: Thames and Hudson.

Veiteberg, J. (2005) *Craft in Transition*. Bergen: Kunsthogskoleni Bergen.

Willcox, D. J. (1998) *Body Jewellery: International Perspectives*. London: Pitman.

Youngs, S. (1989) *The Work of Angels: Masterpieces of Celtic Metalwork 6th–9th Centuries* AD. London: British Museum Publications.

FURTHER READING AND LINKS

BOOKS

Arkhipov, V. (2006) *Home-Made. Contemporary Russian Folk Artefacts*. London: FUEL.

Bury, S. (1991) *Jewellery 1789–1950: the International Era*. Vols 1 and 2. New York: The Antique Collectors Club.

Buszek, M. F. ed. (2011) *Extra/Ordinary*, Durham/London: Duke University Press

Cherry, N. (2008) *Masters and Protégés: Contemporary British Jewellery*. Birmingham: Birmingham City University.

Cochrane, G. ed. (2007) *Smart Works: Design and the Handmade*. Sydney: Powerhouse Publishing.

den Basten, E. (2011) *On Jewellery*. Stuttgart: Arnoldsche.

den Basten, L. and Gaspar, M. eds. (2009) *Skill. Think Tank*.

Findeis, K. (2007) *On Location, Making Stories: Siting, Citing, Sighting*. Sydney: Jewellers and Metalsmiths Group of Australia.

Gauntlett, D. (2012) *Making is Connecting*. Cambridge: Polity.

Joris, Y. G. J. M. ed. (2000) *Jewels of Mind and Mentality*. 's Hertogenbosch: Museum of Contemporary Art.

Maryon, H. (1971) *Techniques of Metalwork and Enamelling*. New York: Dover.

McFadden, D. R. and Sims, L. S. (2010) *Dead or Alive*. New York: Museum of Arts and Design.

Newell, L. B. (2007) *Out of the Ordinary: Spectacular Craft*. London: V & A Publications/ Crafts Council.

Petry, M. (2011) *The Art of Not Making*. London: Thames and Hudson.

Seki, A. ed. (2005). *One Hundred Years of Jewellery in Japan: 1850–1950*. Tokyo: Bijutsu.

Tallis, R. (2003) *The Hand: A Philosophical Inquiry into Human Being*. Edinburgh: Edinburgh University Press.

Untracht, O. (1982) *Jewelry Concepts and Technology*. New York: Doubleday.

Von Neumann, R. (1972) *The Design and Creation of Jewelry*. Radnor PA: Chilton Books.

JOURNALS

American Craft. Minneapolis: American Crafts Council

Crafts. London: The Crafts Council

Design and Culture. Oxford: Berg

The Design Journal. Oxford: Berg

The Journal of Modern Craft. Oxford: Berg

Metalsmith. Bethel, CT: Society of North American Goldsmiths

Online only:

AN Magazine: www.a-n.co.uk

ASSOCIATIONS

Art Jewelry Forum: www.artjewelryforum.org

Associaçao Portuguesa de Joalharia Contemporanea: www.pin.pt

Association for Contemporary Jewellery: www.acj.org.uk

Associazione Gioello Contemporaneo: www.agc-it.org

Forum für Schmuck und Design: www.ffsd.de

Jewellers and Metalsmiths Group of Australia: www.jmgawa.com.au

Society of North American Goldsmiths: www.snagmetalsmith.org

ONLINE ORGANISATIONS

Klimt02 – an online gallery, exhibitions and galleries list, forum for jewellery artists: www.Klimt02.net

Ganoksin – an online source of technical and other information for students and professionals: www.ganoksin.com

CAREERS INFORMATION

www.creative-choice.co.uk

INDEX

A

advertising 74, 76–78
alchemy 92
amber 64
Smith, Art 6
Anima 92-95
Arnheim, Rudolf 47
Art Nouveau 6
Arts & Crafts movement 6

B

bangle 116–118
Barratt, Krome 14
Berlin Iron Work 6
bracelet 34, 41, 106
Britton, Helen 22–27, 80, 123
Bronger, Sigurd 28–31, 124
brooches 22, 34, 42–43, 46, 73–74, 98, 100, 103, 105–108

C

Calder, Alexander 6
Cellini, Benvenuto 6
Central School of Art and Design 6
Chang, Peter 32–35, 125
China 74, 77, 116
colour 24, 61, 54, 76, 99
Computer Aided Design 14, 17, 38, 74
consciousness 42, 45–48, 50, 52, 70, 72, 75
copper 56, 73, 118
Corvaja, Giovanni 36–41, 126
Cottrell, Simon 42–49, 127
Crafts Council 10
culture 22, 58, 62–66, 74, 114
Cuyàs, Ramon Puig 50–55, 128

D

Dalí, Salvador 6
Davie, Alan 6
Dormer, Peter 10

D

Dürer, Albrecht 6
drawing 13, 22, 26, 32, 34, 38, 42, 50, 52, 56, 62, 74, 78, 86, 90–91, 94, 98, 110

E

Edison, Thomas 16
education 17–18
Eichenberg, Iris 56–61, 129
electroforming 73
electronic components 74, 76–78
Emin, Tracey 18–19
Estés, Clarissa Pinkola, 87

F

Freud, Lucian 16
fur 68, 70–73

G

geometry 110–112
globalisation 74, 76–78
gold 38, 41, 45, 56, 90–91, 104, 111–112

H

Hilliard, Nicholas 6
Hogarth 6
Holbein the Younger 6
Hughes, Graham 10

I

Industrial Revolution 6
Izawa, Yoko 62–67, 130

J

Jewellery Industry Innovation Centre 17
John, Augustus 16
de Jong, Rian 68–73, 131
Juen, Lisa 74–79, 132
Jung, Carl Gustav 92

K

Kant, Immanuel 19
Kent Institute of Art and Design 63

M

making 43, 50, 52, 54, 74–75, 80, 98–99, 100
Mälk, Kadri 80–85, 133
metals 6, 9, 13, 36, 104, 106, 110, 114, 115, 118
metaphor 50, 54, 74
Metzinger, Thomas 48
mercury 104, 106
McCaig, Judy 56, 86–91, 134
Moholy-Nagy, László 6
music 34, 50–51

N

nature 32, 34, 43–44, 54, 61, 77–78, 80, 88, 90, 98, 100, 104,
necklace 22, 31, 100, 106, 112
Nisslmüller, Manfred 106

O

O'Toole, Dr Chris 14

P

Pallasmaa, Juhani 19
parameters 43, 45–48
de Patta, Margaret 6
pendant 52–54
perception 42, 45, 49
Peters, Ruudt 92–97, 135
Picasso, Pablo 6, 16
Pietro Selvatico Institute of Art 110–111
Pinchuk, Natalya 56, 98–103, 136
plastics 17, 22–26, 32, 34
Plotkin 16
printmaking 32, 86, 91

proportions 100, 108
Pye, David 13

R

recycling 9, 32
ring 100, 104, 106, 108–109, 116–118
Robinson, Sir Ken 18
Royal College of Art 63

S

Schön, Donald 17
sculpture 32, 91
Second World War 10
Sennett, Richard 16–17, 50
Skubic, Peter 104–109, 137
stainless steel 10, 78, 104–106

T

teapot 70
Theatre of Movement 10
Tolstoy, Leo 6
Turner, Ralph 10

V

Visintin, Graziano 110–113, 138

W

Warhol, Andy 10
wax 92, 94–96
Wilson, Frank 19
Witch of Portobello 121
Wolverhampton Steel Ware 6

Y

Yamada, Mizuko 114–119, 139

PICTURE CREDITS

HELEN BRITTON
All photos by the artist, except "Bleached" necklace, "Crash" ring and "Daytime" brooch, where photographer was Simon Bielander

SIGURD BRONGER
All photos by the artist

PETER CHANG
All photos by the artist

GIOVANNI CORVAJA
All photos by the artist

SIMON COTTRELL
All photos by the artist

RAMON PUIG CUYÀS
All photos by the artist

IRIS EICHENBERG
All photos by Dave Rollins

YOKO IZAWA
Photos of "Inro" rings and "Petal" necklace by the artist
Photo of "Dew Drops" necklace by Nick Jell
All other photos by David Buck

RIAN DE JONG
All photos by the artist

LISA JUEN
All photos by the artist

KADRI MÄLK
All photos by Tiit Rammul

JUDY MCCAIG
Process photos by the artist, and photos of finished pieces by Gonzalo Cáceres

RUUDT PETERS
All photos by Rob Versluys, Amsterdam

NATALYA PINCHUK
All photos by the artist
Photo of "2.10" brooch courtesy of Charon Kransen Arts
Photo of "14.09" brooch courtesy of Rob Koudijs Galerie

PETER SKUBIC
All photos by Petra Zimmermann, Vienna

GRAZIANO VISINTIN
All photos from the Graziano Visintin Archive

MIZUKO YAMADA
All photos by Toshihide Kajihara